Y0-EGB-508

Microsoft®

Access 2000

Illustrated Brief Edition

Lisa Friedrichsen

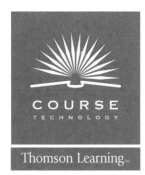

COURSE
TECHNOLOGY

Thomson Learning™

ONE MAIN STREET, CAMBRIDGE, MA 02142

Australia • Canada • Denmark • Japan • Mexico • New Zealand • Philippines
Puerto Rico • Singapore • South Africa • Spain • United Kingdom • United States

Senior Product Manager:	**Kathryn Schooling**
Product Manager:	**Jennifer A. Duffy**
Associate Product Manager:	**Emily Heberlein**
Contributing Author:	**Elizabeth Eisner Reding**
Production Editor:	**Elena Montillo**
Developmental Editor:	**Rachel Biheller Bunin**
Composition House:	**GEX, Inc.**
QA Manuscript Reviewer:	**Nicole Ashton, Jeff Schwartz, Alex White**
Text Designer:	**Joseph Lee, Joseph Lee Designs**
Cover Designer:	**Doug Goodman, Doug Goodman Designs**

Trademarks

Course Technology and the Open Book logo are registered trademarks of Course Technology.

Illustrated Projects and the Illustrated Series are trademarks of Course Technology.

Some of the product names and company names used in this book have been used for identification purposes only and may be trademarks or registered trademarks of their respective manufacturers and sellers.

Disclaimer

Course Technology reserves the right to revise this publication and make changes from time to time in its content without notice.

For more information contact:
Course Technology
One Main Street
Cambridge, MA 02142

ISBN 0-7600-6069-X

Printed in the United States of America

2 3 4 5 6 7 8 9 BM 04 03 02 01 00

The Illustrated Series Offers the Entire Package for your Microsoft Office 2000 Needs

Office 2000 MOUS Certification Coverage

The Illustrated Series offers a growing number of Microsoft-approved titles that cover the objectives required to pass the Office 2000 MOUS (Microsoft Office User Specialist) exams. After studying with any of the approved Illustrated titles (see list on inside cover), you will have mastered the Core and Expert skills necessary to pass any Office 2000 MOUS exam. In addition, **Access 2000 MOUS Certification Objectives** at the end of the book map to where specific MOUS skills can be found in each lesson and where students can find additional practice.

Helpful New Features

The Illustrated Series responded to customer feedback by adding a **Project Files list** at the back of the book for easy reference, changing the red font in the Steps to green for easier reading, and adding new Conceptual lessons to units to give students the extra information they need when learning Office 2000.

New Exciting Case and Innovative On-Line Companion

There is an exciting new case study used throughout our textbooks, a fictitious company called MediaLoft, designed to be "real-world" in nature by introducing the kinds of activities that students will encounter when working with Microsoft Office 2000. The **MediaLoft Web site**, available at www.course.com/illustrated/medialoft, is an innovative Student Online Companion which enhances and augments the printed page by bringing students onto the Web for a dynamic and continually updated learning experience. The MediaLoft site mirrors the case study used throughout the book, creating a real-world intranet site for this chain of bookstore cafés. This Companion is used to complete the WebWorks exercise in each unit of this book, and to allow students to become familiar with the business application of an intranet site.

Enhance Any Illustrated Text with these Exciting Products!

Course CBT

Enhance your students' Office 2000 classroom learning experience with self-paced computer-based training on CD-ROM. Course CBT engages students with interactive multimedia and hands-on simulations that reinforce and complement the concepts and skills covered in the textbook. All the content is aligned with the MOUS program, making it a great preparation tool for the certification exams. Course CBT also includes extensive pre- and post-assessments that test students' mastery of skills.

SAM 2000

How well do your students *really* know Microsoft Office? SAM 2000 is a performance-based testing program that measures students' proficiency in Microsoft Office 2000. SAM 2000 is available for Office 2000 in either a live or simulated environment. You can use SAM 2000 to place students into or out of courses, monitor their performance throughout a course, and help prepare them for the MOUS certification exams.

Create Your Ideal Course Package with CourseKits™

If one book doesn't offer all the coverage you need, create a course package that does. With Course Technology's CourseKits—our mix-and-match approach to selecting texts—you have the freedom to combine products from more than one series. When you choose any two or more Course Technology products for one course, we'll discount the price and package them together so your students can pick up one convenient bundle at the bookstore.

For more information about any of these offerings or other Course Technology products, contact your sales representative or visit our web site at:

www.course.com

Preface

Welcome to *Microsoft Access 2000—Illustrated Brief Edition*. This highly visual book offers users a hands-on introduction to basic aspects of Microsoft Access 2000 and also serves as an excellent reference for future use. If you would like additional coverage of Microsoft Access 2000, we also offer *Microsoft Access 2000—Illustrated Introductory*, a logical continuation of the Brief Edition.

▶ Organization and Coverage
This text contains four units that cover basic Access skills. In these units, students learn how to create, format, and use Access databases, including tables, queries, forms, and reports.

▶ About this Approach
What makes the Illustrated approach so effective at teaching software skills? It's quite simple. Each skill is presented on two facing pages, with the step-by-step instructions on the left page, and large screen illustrations on the right. Students can focus on a single skill without having to turn the page. This unique design makes information extremely accessible and easy to absorb, and provides a great reference for after the course is over. This hands-on approach also makes it ideal for both self-paced or instructor-led classes.

Each lesson, or "information display," contains the following elements:

Each 2-page spread focuses on a single skill.

Clear step-by-step directions explain how to complete the specific task, with what students are to type in green. When students follow the numbered steps, they quickly learn how each procedure is performed and what the results will be.

Concise text that introduces the basic principles discussed in the lesson. Procedures are easier to learn when concepts fit into a framework.

Access 2000

Viewing the Database Window

When you start Access and open a database, the database window displays common Windows elements such as a title bar, menu bar, and toolbar. Clicking the Objects or Groups buttons on the Objects bar alternatively expands and collapses that section of the database window. If all the objects don't display in the expanded section, click the small arrow at the top or bottom of the section to scroll the list. The Objects area displays the seven types of objects that can be accessed by clicking the object type you want. The Groups area displays other commonly used files and folders, such as the Favorites folder. ▶ John explores the MediaLoft-A database.

Steps

1. **Look at each of the Access window elements shown in Figure A-7**
   The Objects bar on the left side of the database window displays the seven object types. The other elements of the database window are summarized in Table A-3. Because the Tables object is selected, the buttons you need to create a new table or to work with the existing table are displayed in the MediaLoft-A Database window.

QuickTip
Your menu commands may look different depending on which window or object is in use.

2. **Click File on the menu bar**
   The File menu contains commands for opening a new or existing database, saving a database in a variety of formats, and printing. The menu commands vary depending on which window or database object is currently in use.

3. **Point to Edit on the menu bar, point to View, point to Insert, point to Tools, point to Window, point to Help, move the pointer off the menu, then press [Esc] twice**
   All menus close when you press [Esc]. Pressing [Esc] a second time deselects the menu.

4. **Point to the New button ▢ on the Database toolbar**
   Pointing to a toolbar button causes a descriptive ScreenTip to automatically appear, providing a short description of the button. The buttons on the toolbars represent the most commonly used Access features. Toolbar buttons change just as menu options change depending on which window and database object are currently in use.

5. **Point to the Open button ▢ on the Database toolbar, then point to the Save button ▢ on the Database toolbar**
   Sometimes toolbar buttons or menu options are dimmed which means that they are currently unavailable. For example, the Save button is dimmed because it doesn't make sense to save the MediaLoft-A database right now because you haven't made any changes to it yet.

6. **Click Queries on the Objects bar**
   The query object window provides several ways to create a new query and displays the names of previously created queries, as shown in Figure A-8. There are three previously created query objects displayed within the MediaLoft-A Database window.

7. **Click Forms on the Objects bar, then click Reports on the Objects bar**
   The MediaLoft-A database contains the Customers table, three queries, a customer entry form, and three reports.

▶ CLUES TO USE
Viewing objects
You can change the way you view the objects in the database window by clicking the last four buttons on the toolbar. You can view the objects as Large Icons ▢, Small Icons ▢, in a List ▢ (this is the default view), and with Details ▢. The Details view shows a longer description of the object, as well as the date the object was last modified and the date it was originally created.

▶ ACCESS A-8 **GETTING STARTED WITH ACCESS 2000**

Hints as well as trouble-shooting advice, right where you need it — next to the step itself.

Clues to Use boxes provide concise information that either expands on one component of the major lesson skill or describes an independent task that is in some way related to the major lesson skill.

Other Features

The two-page lesson format featured in this book provides the new user with a powerful learning experience. Additionally, this book contains the following features:

Every lesson features large-size, full-color representations of what the students' screen should look like after completing the numbered steps.

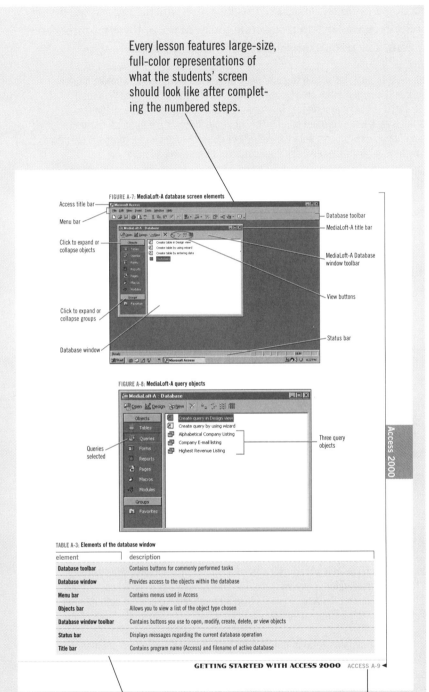

FIGURE A-7: MediaLoft-A database screen elements

Access title bar
Menu bar
Click to expand or collapse objects
Click to expand or collapse groups
Database window

Database toolbar
MediaLoft-A title bar
MediaLoft-A Database window toolbar
View buttons
Status bar

FIGURE A-8: MediaLoft-A query objects

Queries selected

Three query objects

TABLE A-3: Elements of the database window

element	description
Database toolbar	Contains buttons for commonly performed tasks
Database window	Provides access to the objects within the database
Menu bar	Contains menus used in Access
Objects bar	Allows you to view a list of the object type chosen
Database window toolbar	Contains buttons you use to open, modify, create, delete, or view objects
Status bar	Displays messages regarding the current database operation
Title bar	Contains program name (Access) and filename of active database

GETTING STARTED WITH ACCESS 2000 ACCESS A-9 ◄

Quickly accessible summaries of key terms, toolbar buttons, or keyboard alternatives connected with the lesson material. Students can refer easily to this information when working on their own projects at a later time.

The page numbers are designed like a road map. Access indicates the Access section, A indicates the first unit, and 9 indicates the page within the unit.

▶ **MOUS Certification Coverage**
Each unit opener has a ⌐MOUS⌐ next to it to indicate where Microsoft Office User Specialist (MOUS) skills are covered. In addition, there is a MOUS appendix which contains a grid that maps to where specific Core Access MOUS skills can be found in each lesson and where students can find additional practice. This book makes up the first four units of *Microsoft Access 2000-Illustrated Introductory, 0-7600-6070-3*, which thoroughly prepares students to learn the Core skills needed to pass the Access 2000 MOUS exam. *Microsoft Access-Illustrated Complete, 0-7600-6072-X*, teaches students the Expert skills needed for the Access 2000 Expert MOUS exam.

▶ **Real-World Case**
The case study used throughout the textbook, a fictitious company called MediaLoft, is designed to be "'real-world" in nature and introduces the kinds of activities that students will encounter when working with Microsoft Access 2000. With a real-world case, the process of solving problems will be more meaningful to students.
Students can also enhance their skills by completing the Web Works exercises in each unit by going to the innovative Student Online Companion, available at **www.course.com/illustrated/medialoft**. The MediaLoft site mirrors the case study by acting as the company's intranet site, further allowing students to become familiar with applicable business scenarios.

▶ **End of Unit Material**
Each unit concludes with a Concepts Review that tests students' understanding of what they learned in the unit. The Concepts Review is followed by a Skills Review, which provides students with additional hands-on practice of the skills. The Skills Review is followed by Independent Challenges, which pose case problems for students to solve. At least one Independent Challenge in each unit asks students to use the World Wide Web to solve the problem as indicated by a Web Work icon. The Visual Workshops that follow the Independent Challenges help students develop critical thinking skills. Students are shown completed Web pages or screens and are asked to recreate them from scratch.

Instructor's Resource Kit

The Instructor's Resource Kit is Course Technology's way of putting the resources and information needed to teach and learn effectively into your hands. With an integrated array of teaching and learning tools that offers you and your students a broad range of technology-based instructional options, we believe this kit represents the highest quality and most cutting edge resources available to instructors today. Many of these resources are available at www.course.com. The resources available with this book are:

MediaLoft Web site   Available at **www.course.com/illustrated/medialoft**, this innovative Student Online Companion enhances and augments the printed page by bringing students onto the Web for a dynamic and continually updated learning experience. The MediaLoft site mirrors the case study used throughout the book, creating a real-world intranet site for this fictitious company, a national chain of bookstore cafés. This Companion is used to complete the WebWorks exercise in each unit of this book, and to allow students to become familiar with the business application of an intranet site.

Instructor's Manual   Available as an electronic file, the Instructor's Manual is quality-assurance tested and includes unit overviews, detailed lecture topics for each unit with teaching tips, an Upgrader's Guide, solutions to all lessons and end-of-unit material, and extra Independent Challenges. The Instructor's Manual is available on the Instructor's Resource Kit CD-ROM, or you can download it from **www.course.com**.

Course Faculty Online Companion   You can browse this textbook's password-protected site to obtain the Instructor's Manual, Solution Files, Project Files, and any updates to the text. Contact your Customer Service Representative for the site address and password.

Project Files   Project Files contain all of the data that students will use to complete the lessons and end-of-unit material. A Readme file includes instructions for using the files. Adopters of this text are granted the right to install the Project Files on any standalone computer or network. The Project Files are available on the Instructor's Resource Kit CD-ROM, the Review Pack, and can also be downloaded from www.course.com.

Solution Files   Solution Files contain every file students are asked to create or modify in the lessons and end-of-unit material. A Help file on the Instructor's Resource Kit includes information for using the Solution Files.

CyberClass   CyberClass is a web-based tool designed for on-campus or distance learning. Use it to enhance how you currently run your class by posting assignments and your course syllabus or holding online office hours. Or, use it for your distance learning course, and offer mini-lectures, conduct online discussion groups, or give your mid-term exam. For more information, visit our Web site at: **www.course.com/products/cyberclass/index.html**.

WebCT   WebCT is a tool used to create Web-based educational environments and also uses WWW browsers as the interface for the course-building environment. The site is hosted on your school campus, allowing complete control over the information. WebCT has its own internal communication system, offering internal e-mail, a Bulletin Board, and a Chat room.

Course Technology offers pre-existing supplemental information to help in your WebCT class creation, such as a suggested Syllabus, Lecture Notes, Figures in the Book / Course Presenter, Student Downloads, and Test Banks in which you can schedule an exam, create reports, and more.

Contents

 ▶ Access 2000

Contents

Getting
Started with Access 2000

Objectives

- MOUS ▶ **Define database software**
- MOUS ▶ **Learn database terminology**
- ▶ **Start Access and open a database**
- MOUS ▶ **View the database window**
- MOUS ▶ **Navigate records**
- MOUS ▶ **Enter records**
- MOUS ▶ **Edit records**
- MOUS ▶ **Preview and print a datasheet**
- MOUS ▶ **Get Help and exit Access**

In this unit, you will learn the purpose, advantages, and terminology of
Microsoft Access 2000, a database software. You will also learn how to
open a database and how to use the different elements of the Access
window. You'll learn how to get help. You'll learn how to navigate
through a database, enter and update data, and preview and print data.
John Kim is the director of shipping at MediaLoft, a nationwide
chain of bookstore cafés that sells books, music, and videos. Recently,
MediaLoft switched to Access from an index card system for storing and
maintaining customer information. John will use Access to enter and
maintain this critical information for MediaLoft.

Defining Database Software

Microsoft Access 2000 is a database software program that runs on Windows. **Database software** is used to manage data that can be organized into lists of related information, such as customers, products, vendors, employees, projects, or sales. Many small companies record customer, inventory, and sales information in a spreadsheet program such as Microsoft Excel. While this electronic format is more productive than writing information on index cards, Excel still lacks many of the database advantages provided by Access. Refer to Table A-1 for a comparison of the two programs. ◢◣◤ John reviews the advantages that database software has over a manual index card system.

Data entry is faster and easier
Before inexpensive microcomputers, small businesses used manual paper systems, such as index cards, to record each customer, sale, and inventory item as illustrated in Figure A-1. Using an electronic database such as Access, you can create on-screen data entry forms, which make managing a database easier, more accurate, and more efficient than using index cards.

Information retrieval is faster and easier
Retrieving information on an index card system is tedious because the cards have to be physically handled, sorted, and stored. Also, one error in filing can cause serious retrieval problems later. With Access you can quickly search for, display, and print information on customers, sales, or inventory.

Information can be viewed and sorted in multiple ways
A card system allows you to sort the cards in only one order, unless the cards are duplicated for a second arrangement. Customer and inventory cards were generally sorted alphabetically by name. Sales index cards were usually sorted by date. In this system, complete customer and product information was recorded on each of their individual cards as well as on the corresponding sale cards. This quickly compromises data accuracy. Access allows you to view or sort the information from one or more subjects simultaneously. For example, you might want to know all the customers who purchased a particular product or all the products purchased by a particular customer. A change made to the data in one view of Access is automatically updated in every other view or report.

Information is more secure
Index cards can be torn, misplaced, and stolen. There is no password required to read them, and a disaster, such as a flood or fire, could completely destroy them. You can back up an Access database file on a regular basis and store the file at an offsite location. You can also password protect data so only those users with appropriate security clearances can view or manipulate the data.

Information can be shared among several users
An index card system is limited to those users who can physically reach it. If one user keeps a card for an extended period of time, then others cannot use or update that information. Access databases are inherently multiuser. More than one person can be entering, updating, and using the data at the same time.

Duplicate data entry is minimized
The index card system requires that the user duplicate the customer and product information on each sales card. With Access, you only need to enter each piece of information once. Figure A-2 shows a possible structure for an Access database to record sales.

FIGURE A-1: Using index cards to organize sales data

FIGURE A-2: Using Access, an electronic relational database, to organize sales data

TABLE A-1: Comparing Excel to Access

feature	Excel	Access
Layout	Provides a natural tabular layout for easy data entry	Provides a spreadsheet "view" as well as forms which arrange data in a variety of ways
Storage	Limited to approximately 65,000 records per sheet	Able to store any number of records up to 2 gigabytes
Linked tables	Manages single lists of information	Allows links between lists of information to reduce data entry redundancy
Reporting	Limited to a spreadsheet printout	Provides sophisticated reporting features such as multiple headers and footers and calculations on groups of records
Security	Very limited	Each user can be given access to only the records and fields they need
Multiuser capabilities	Does not allow multiple users to simultaneously enter and update data	Allows multiple users to simultaneously enter and update data
Data entry screens	Provides limited data entry screens	Provides the ability to create extensive data entry screens called forms

Learning Database Terminology

To become familiar with Access, you need to understand basic database terminology. John reviews the terms and concepts that define a database.

Details

A **database** is a collection of information associated with a topic (for example, sales of products to customers). The smallest piece of information in a database is called a **field**, or category of information, such as the customer's name, city, state, or phone number. A **key field** is a field that contains unique information for each record. A group of related fields, such as all demographic information for one customer, is called a **record**. In Access, a collection of records for a single subject, such as all of the customer records, is called a **table**, as shown in Figure A-3.

An Access database is a **relational database**, in which more than one table, such as the Customer, Sales, and Product tables, can share information. The term "relational database" comes from the fact that two tables are linked, or related, by a common field.

Tables, therefore, are the most important **object** in an Access database because they contain all of the data within the database. An Access database may also contain six other objects, which serve to enhance the usability and value of the data. The objects in an Access database are tables, queries, forms, reports, pages, macros, and modules, and they are summarized in Table A-2.

Data can be entered and edited in four of the objects: tables, queries, forms, and pages. The relationship between tables, queries, forms, and reports is shown in Figure A-4. Regardless of how the data is entered, it is physically stored in a table object. Data can be printed from a table, query, form, page, or report object. The macro and module objects are used to provide additional database productivity and automation features. All of the objects (except for the page objects, which are used to create Web pages) are stored in one database file.

TABLE A-2: Access objects and their purpose

object	purpose
Table	Contains all of the raw data within the database in a spreadsheet-like view; tables can be linked with a common field to share information and therefore minimize data redundancy
Query	Provides a spreadsheet-like view of the data similar to tables, but a query can be designed to provide the user with a subset of fields or records from one or more tables; queries are created when a user has a "question" about the data in the database
Form	Provides an easy-to-use data entry screen, which generally shows only one record at a time
Report	Provides a professional printout of data that may contain enhancements such as headers, footers, and calculations on groups of records
Page	Creates Web pages from Access objects as well as provides Web page connectivity features to an Access database, also called Data Access Page
Macro	Stores a collection of keystrokes or commands, such as printing several reports or displaying a toolbar when a form opens
Module	Stores Visual Basic programming code that extends the functions and automated processes of Access

FIGURE A-3: Tables contain fields and records

FIGURE A-4: The relationship between Access objects

Starting Access and Opening a Database

You can start Access by clicking the Access icon on the Windows desktop or on the Microsoft Office Shortcut Bar. Since not all computers will provide a shortcut icon on the desktop or display the Office Shortcut Bar, you can always find Access by clicking the Start button on the taskbar, pointing to Programs, and then choosing Access from the Programs menu. You can open a database from within Access or by finding the database file on the desktop, in My Computer, or in Windows Explorer, and then opening it. ✎ John starts Access and opens the MediaLoft-A database.

1. Click the **Start button** 🏁 Start on the taskbar

The Start button is in the lower-left corner of the taskbar. You can use the Start menu to start any program on your computer.

2. Point to **Programs**

Access is generally located on the Programs menu. All the programs, or applications, stored on your computer can be found here.

3. Click **Microsoft Access**

Access opens and displays the Access dialog box, from which you can start a new database or open an existing file.

4. Insert your Project Disk in the appropriate disk drive

To complete the units in this book, you need a Project Disk. See your instructor or technical support person for assistance.

5. Click **More Files**, then click **OK**

The Open dialog box appears, as shown in Figure A-5. Depending on the databases and folders stored on your computer, your dialog box may look slightly different.

6. Click the **Look in list arrow**, then click **3½ Floppy (A:)**

A list of the files on your Project Disk appears in the Open dialog box.

7. Click the **MediaLoft-A** database file, click **Open**, then click the **Maximize button** on the title bar if the Access window does not fill the screen

The MediaLoft-A database opens as shown in Figure A-6.

> **Trouble?**
>
> If you can't locate Microsoft Access on the Programs menu, point to the Microsoft Office group and look for Access there.

> **QuickTip**
>
> Make a copy of your Project Disk before you use it.

> **Trouble?**
>
> These lessons assume your Project Disk is in drive A. If you are using a different drive, substitute that drive for drive A in the steps.

CLUES TO USE

Personalized toolbars and menus in Office 2000

Office 2000 toolbars and menus modify themselves to your working style. The toolbars you see when you first start a program include the most frequently used buttons. To locate a button not visible on a toolbar, click the More Buttons button at the end of the toolbar to see the list of additional toolbar buttons. As you work, the program adds the buttons you use to the visible toolbars and moves the buttons you haven't used in a while to the More Buttons list. Similarly, menus adjust to your work habits. Short menus appear when you first click a menu command. To view additional menu commands, point to the double-arrow at the bottom of the menu, leave the pointer on the menu name after you've clicked the menu, or double-click the menu name. If you select a command that's not on the short menu, the program automatically adds it to the short menus. You can return personalized toolbars and menus to their original settings by clicking Tools on the menu bar, then clicking Customize. On the Options tab in the Customize dialog box, click Reset my usage data, click Yes to close the alert box, then close the Customize dialog box. Resetting usage data erases changes made automatically to your menus and toolbars. It does not affect the options you customize.

FIGURE A-5: Open dialog box

The folders on your computer will vary

Look in list arrow

FIGURE A-6: MediaLoft-A database

Objects bar

Media Loft-A Database window

Access window is maximized

More Buttons button

Viewing the Database Window

When you start Access and open a database, the **database window** displays common Windows elements such as a title bar, menu bar, and toolbar. Clicking the Objects or Groups buttons on the Objects bar alternatively expands and collapses that section of the database window. If all the objects don't display in the expanded section, click the small arrow at the top or bottom of the section to scroll the list. The **Objects** area displays the seven types of objects that can be accessed by clicking the object type you want. The **Groups** area displays other commonly used files and folders, such as the Favorites folder. John explores the MediaLoft-A database.

Steps

1. **Look at each of the Access window elements shown in Figure A-7**
   The Objects bar on the left side of the database window displays the seven object types. The other elements of the database window are summarized in Table A-3. Because the Tables object is selected, the buttons you need to create a new table or to work with the existing table are displayed in the MediaLoft-A Database window.

2. **Click File on the menu bar**
   The File menu contains commands for opening a new or existing database, saving a database in a variety of formats, and printing. The menu commands vary depending on which window or database object is currently in use.

3. **Point to Edit on the menu bar, point to View, point to Insert, point to Tools, point to Window, point to Help, move the pointer off the menu, then press [Esc] twice**
   All menus close when you press [Esc]. Pressing [Esc] a second time deselects the menu.

4. **Point to the New button ☐ on the Database toolbar**
   Pointing to a toolbar button causes a descriptive **ScreenTip** to automatically appear, providing a short description of the button. The buttons on the toolbars represent the most commonly used Access features. Toolbar buttons change just as menu options change depending on which window and database object are currently in use.

5. **Point to the Open button ☞ on the Database toolbar, then point to the Save button ☐ on the Database toolbar**
   Sometimes toolbar buttons or menu options are dimmed which means that they are currently unavailable. For example, the Save button is dimmed because it doesn't make sense to save the MediaLoft-A database right now because you haven't made any changes to it yet.

6. **Click Queries on the Objects bar**
   The query object window provides several ways to create a new query and displays the names of previously created queries, as shown in Figure A-8. There are three previously created query objects displayed within the MediaLoft-A Database window.

7. **Click Forms on the Objects bar, then click Reports on the Objects bar**
   The MediaLoft-A database contains the Customers table, three queries, a customer entry form, and three reports.

Viewing objects

You can change the way you view the objects in the database window by clicking the last four buttons on the toolbar. You can view the objects as Large Icons ⬛, Small Icons ⬛, in a List ⬛ (this is the default view), and with Details ⬛. The Details view shows a longer description of the object, as well as the date the object was last modified and the date it was originally created.

FIGURE A-7: MediaLoft-A database screen elements

Access title bar
Menu bar
Click to expand or collapse objects
Click to expand or collapse groups
Database window

Database toolbar
MediaLoft-A title bar
MediaLoft-A Database window toolbar
View buttons
Status bar

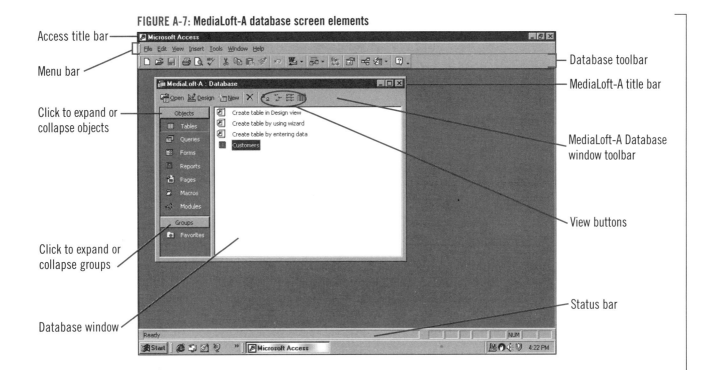

FIGURE A-8: MediaLoft-A query objects

Queries selected
Three query objects

TABLE A-3: Elements of the database window

element	description
Database toolbar	Contains buttons for commonly performed tasks
Database window	Provides access to the objects within the database
Menu bar	Contains menus used in Access
Objects bar	Allows you to view a list of the object type chosen
Database window toolbar	Contains buttons you use to open, modify, create, delete, or view objects
Status bar	Displays messages regarding the current database operation
Title bar	Contains program name (Access) and filename of active database

Navigating Records

Your ability to navigate through the fields and records of a database is key to your productivity and success with the database. You navigate through the information in **Navigation mode** in the table's **datasheet**, a spreadsheet-like grid that displays fields as columns and records as rows. John opens the database and reviews the table containing information about MediaLoft's customers.

Steps

QuickTip
You can also double-click an object to open it.

1. **Click Tables on the Objects bar, click Customers, then click the Open button 🖼 on the MediaLoft-A Database window toolbar**
   The datasheet for the Customers table opens, as shown in Figure A-9. The datasheet contains 27 customer records with 13 fields of information for each record. **Field names** are listed at the top of each column. The number of the selected record in the datasheet is displayed in the **Specific Record box** at the bottom of the datasheet window. Depending on the size of your monitor and the resolution of your computer system, you may see a different number of fields. If all of the fields don't display, you can scroll to the right to see the rest.

2. **Press [Tab] to move to Sprint**
   Sprint is the entry in the second field, Company, of the first record.

3. **Press [Enter]**
   The data, Aaron, is selected in the third field, First. Pressing either [Tab] or [Enter] moves the focus to the next field. **Focus** refers to which field would be edited if you started typing.

4. **Press [↓]**
   The focus moves to the Kelsey entry in the First field of the second record. The **current record symbol** in the **record selector box** also identifies which record you are navigating. The Next Record and Previous Record **navigation buttons** can also be used to navigate the datasheet.

5. **Press [Ctrl][End]**
   The focus moves to the last field of the last record. You can also use the Last Record navigation button to move to the last record.

6. **Press [Ctrl][Home]**
   The focus moves to the first field of the first record. You can also use the First Record navigation button to move to the first record. A complete listing of navigation keystrokes to move the focus between fields and records is shown in Table A-4.

Changing to Edit mode

If you click a field with the mouse pointer instead of pressing the [Tab] or [Enter] to navigate through the datasheet, you change from Navigation mode to **Edit mode**. In Edit mode, Access assumes that you are trying to edit that particular field, so keystrokes such as [Ctrl][End], [Ctrl][Home], [←], and [→] move the insertion point *within* the field. To return to Navigation mode, press [Tab] or [Enter] which moves the focus to the next field, or press [↑] or [↓] which moves the focus to a different record.

FIGURE A-9: Customers datasheet

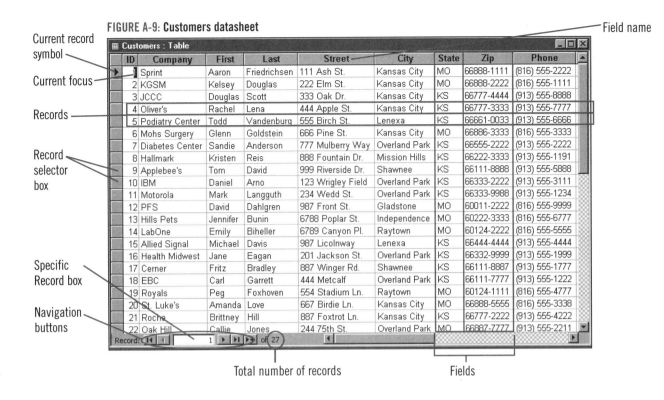

TABLE A-4: Navigation mode keyboard shortcuts

shortcut key	to move to the
[Tab], [Enter] or [→]	Next field of the current record
[Shift][Tab] or [←]	Previous field of the current record
[Home]	First field of the current record
[End]	Last field of the current record
[Ctrl][Home]	First field of the first record
[Ctrl][End]	Last field of the last record
[↑]	Current field of the previous record
[↓]	Current field of the next record
[Ctrl][↑]	Current field of the first record
[Ctrl][↓]	Current field of the last record
[F5]	Specific record

Access 2000

Entering Records

Adding records to a database is a critical task that is usually performed on a daily basis. You can add a new record by clicking the **New Record button** on the Table Datasheet toolbar or by clicking the New Record navigation button. A new record is always added at the end of the datasheet. You can reorder the records in a datasheet by sorting, which you will learn later. John is ready to add two new records in the Customers table. First he maximizes the datasheet window.

Steps

1. **Click the Maximize button on the Customers Table datasheet window title bar**
   Maximizing both the Access and datasheet windows displays the most information possible on the screen and allows you to see more fields and records.

2. **Click the New Record button** ▸ **on the Table Datasheet toolbar, then press [Tab] to move through the ID field and into the Company field**
   The ID field is an **AutoNumber** field, which automatically assigns a new number each time you add a record.

3. **Type CIO, press [Tab], type Lisa, press [Tab], type Lang, press [Tab], type 420 Locust St., press [Tab], type Lenexa, press [Tab], type KS, press [Tab], type 66111-8899, press [Tab], type 9135551189, press [Tab], type 9135551889, press [Tab], type 9/6/69, press [Tab], type lang@cio.com, press [Tab], type 5433.22, then press [Enter]**
   The ID for the record for Lisa Lang is 28. AutoNumber fields should not be used as a counter for how many records you have in a table. Think of the AutoNumber field as an arbitrary but unique number for each record. The value in an AutoNumber field increments by one for each new record and cannot be edited or reused even if the entire record is deleted. The purpose of an AutoNumber field is to uniquely identify each new record. It logs how many records have been added to the datasheet since the creation of the datasheet, and not how many records are currently in the datasheet.

Trouble?

The ID number for the new records may be different in your database.

4. **Enter the new record for Rachel Best shown in the table below**

in field:	type:	in field:	type:
ID	29	Zip	65555-4444
Company	RBB Events	Phone	913-555-2289
First	Rachel	Fax	913-555-2889
Last	Best	Birthdate	8/20/68
Street	500 Sunset Blvd.	Email	Best@rbb.com
City	Manhattan	YTDSales	5998.33
State	KS		

   Compare your updated datasheet with Figure A-10.

FIGURE A-10: Customers table with two new records

Table Datasheet toolbar

Both windows are maximized

New record button

Two new records

New record button

FIGURE A-11: Moving a field

Mouse pointer

Moving datasheet columns

You can reorganize the fields in a datasheet by dragging the field name left or right. Figure A-11 shows how the mouse pointer changes to 🗎, as the Email field is moved to the left. The black vertical line represents the new location between the Fax and Birthdate fields. Release the mouse button when you have appropriately positioned the field.

Editing Records

Updating information in databases is another important daily task required to keep your database current. To change the contents of an existing record, click the field you'd like to change to switch to Edit mode, then type the new information. You can delete any unwanted data by clicking the field and using the [Backspace] and [Delete] keys to delete text to the left and right of the insertion point. Other data entry keystrokes are summarized in Table A-5. ➡ John needs to make some corrections to the datasheet of the Customers table. He starts by correcting an error in the Street field of the first record.

Steps

1. **Press [Ctrl][Home] to move to the first record, click to the right of 111 Ash St. in the Street field, press [Backspace] three times to delete St., then type Dr.**
   When you are editing a record, the **edit record symbol**, which looks like a small pencil, appears in the record selector box to the left of the current record, as shown in Figure A-12.

2. **Click to the right of Hallmark in the Company field in record 8, press [Spacebar], type Cards, then press [↓] to move to the next record**
   You do not need to explicitly save new records or changes to existing records because Access saves the new data as soon as you move to another record or close the data sheet.

3. **Click Shawnee in the City field for record 17, then press [Ctrl]['']**
   The entry changes from "Shawnee" to "Overland Park." [Ctrl]['] inserts the data from the same field in the previous record.

4. **Click to the left of EBC in the Company field for record 18, press [Delete] to remove the E, press [Tab] to move to the next field, then type Doug**
   "Doug" replaces the current entry "Carl" in the First field. Notice the edit record symbol in the record selector box to the left of record 18. Since you are still editing this record, you can undo the changes.

5. **Press [Esc]**
   The Doug entry changes back to Carl. Pressing [Esc] once removes the current field's editing changes.

6. **Press [Esc] again**
   Pressing [Esc] a second time removes all changes made to the record you are currently editing. The company entry is restored to EBC. The ability to use the [Esc] key in edit mode to remove data entry changes is dependent on whether or not you are still editing the record (as evidenced by the edit record symbol to the left of the record). Once you move to another record, the changes are saved, and you return to Navigation mode. In Navigation mode you can no longer use the [Esc] key to remove editing changes, but you can click the **Undo button** 🔙 on the Table Database toolbar to undo the last change you made.

7. **Press [↓] to move to Peg in the First field of record 19, type Peggy, then press [↓] to move to record 20**
   Since you are no longer editing record 19, the [Esc] key has no effect on the last change.

QuickTip

The ScreenTip for the Undo button displays the action you can undo.

8. **Click the Undo button 🔙 on the Table Datasheet toolbar**
   You undo the last edit and Peggy is changed back to Peg. Access only allows you to undo your last action. You can also delete a record directly from the datasheet.

9. **Click the Allied Signal ID 15 Record Selector box, click the Delete Record button 🗙 on the Table Datasheet toolbar, then click Yes to confirm that you want to delete the record**
   You cannot undo a record deletion operation.

FIGURE A-12: Editing records

Edit record
symbol

Insertion
point

TABLE A-5: Edit mode keyboard shortcuts

editing keystroke	action
[Backspace]	Deletes one character to the left of the insertion point
[Delete]	Deletes one character to the right of the insertion point
[F2]	Switches to Edit mode from Navigation mode
[Esc]	Undoes the change to the current field
[Esc][Esc]	Undoes the change to the current record
[F7]	Starts the spell check feature
[Ctrl][']	Inserts the value from the same field in the previous record into the current field
[Ctrl][;]	Inserts the current date in a date field

Resizing datasheet columns

You can resize the width of the field in a datasheet by dragging the thin black line that separates the field names to the left or right. The mouse pointer changes to ✛ as you resize the field to make it wider or narrower. Release the mouse button when you have resized the field.

Previewing and Printing a Datasheet

After entering and editing the records in a table, you can print the datasheet to obtain a hard copy of it. Before printing the datasheet, you should preview it to see how it will look when printed. Often you will want to make adjustments to margins and page orientation. ➡ John is ready to preview and print the datasheet.

Steps 1 2 3 4

QuickTip

If you need your name on the printed solution, enter your name as a new record in the datasheet.

1. **Click the Print Preview button** on the Table Database toolbar
   The datasheet appears as a miniature page in the Print Preview window, as shown in Figure A-14. The Print Preview toolbar provides options for printing, viewing more than one page, and sending the information to Word or Excel.

2. **Click** on the top of the miniature datasheet
   By magnifying this view of the datasheet, you can see its header, which includes the object name, Customers, in the center of the top of the page and the date on the right.

3. **Scroll down to view the bottom of the page**
   The footer displays a page number centered on the bottom.

4. **Click the Two Pages button** on the Print Preview toolbar
   You decide to increase the top margin of the printout.

5. **Click File on the menu bar, then click Page Setup**
   The Page Setup dialog box opens, as shown in Figure A-15. This dialog box provides options for changing margins, removing the headings (the header and footer), and changing page orientation from portrait (default) to landscape on the Page tab.

6. **Double-click 1" in the Top text box, type 2, then click OK**
   The modified datasheet appears in the window. Satisfied with the layout for the printout, you'll print the datasheet and close the Print Preview window.

7. **Click the Print button** on the Print Preview toolbar, then click **Close**
   The datasheet appears on the screen.

Hiding fields

Sometimes you don't need all the fields of a datasheet on a printout. To temporarily hide a field from viewing and therefore from a resulting datasheet printout, click the field name, click Format on the menu bar, and then click Hide Columns. To redisplay the column, click Format, then Unhide Columns. The Unhide Columns dialog box, shown in Figure A-13, opens. The empty columns check boxes indicate the columns that are hidden. Clicking the check boxes will bring the columns back into view on the datasheet.

FIGURE A-13: Unhide Columns dialog box

These fields are currently hidden

FIGURE A-14: Datasheet in print preview (portrait orientation)

Print
Preview
toolbar

Two pages
button

Click to close the
Print Preview window

FIGURE A-15: **Page Setup dialog box**

Click the Page tab for page
orientation options (portrait
vs. landscape)

Getting Help and Exiting Access

When you have finished working in your database, you need to close the object you were working in, such as a table datasheet, and then close the database. To close a table, click Close on the File menu or click the object's Close button located in the upper-right corner of the menu bar. Once you have closed all open objects, you can exit the program. As with most programs, if you try to exit Access and have not yet saved changes to open objects, Access will prompt you to save your changes. You can use the Help system to learn more about the program and get help. ✎ John has finished working with Access for now, so he closes the Customers table and MediaLoft-A database. Before exiting, he learns more about the Help system, and then exits Access.

Steps

1. **Click the Close button for the Customers datasheet**
   The MediaLoft-A database window displays. If you make any structural changes to the datasheet such as moving, resizing, or hiding columns, you will be prompted to save those changes.

2. **Click the Close button for the MediaLoft-A Database, as shown in Figure A-16**
   The MediaLoft-A database is closed, but Access is still running so you could open another database or explore the Help system to learn more about Access at this time.

3. **Click Help on the menu bar, then click Microsoft Access Help**
   The Office Assistant opens and offers to get the help you need. You can further explore some of the concepts you have learned by finding information in the Access Help system. Table A-6 summarizes the options on the Access Help menu, which provides in-depth information on Access features.

4. **Type What is a table, click Search, click Tables: what they are and how they work, then click the graphic as shown in Figure A-17**

5. **Read the information, then click each of the five pages**

6. **Close the Access Help windows**

7. **Click File on the menu bar, then click Exit**
   You have exited Access.

> **Trouble?**
> Do not remove your Project Disk from drive A until you have exited Access.

Shutting down your computer

Never shut off a computer before the screen indicates that it is safe to do so. If you shut off a computer during the initial Windows load process (the screen dis-plays the Windows logo and a cloud background at this time) or before the screen indicates that it is safe to do so, you can corrupt your Windows files.

FIGURE A-16: Closing a database

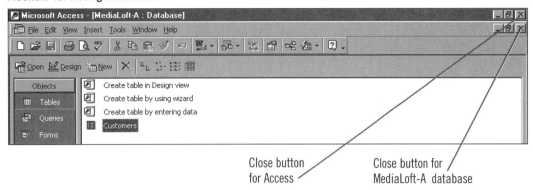

Close button for Access

Close button for MediaLoft-A database

FIGURE A-17: Access Help window

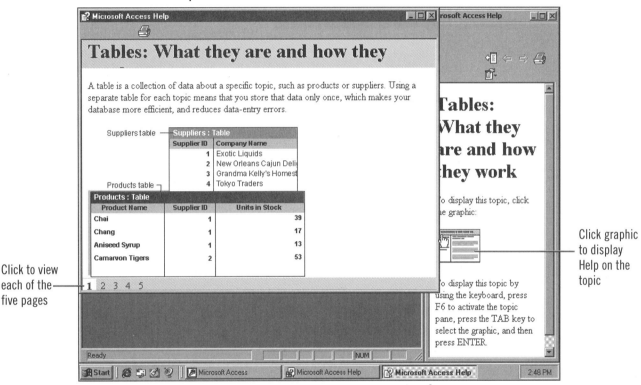

Click to view each of the five pages

Click graphic to display Help on the topic

TABLE A-6: Help menu options

menu option	description
Microsoft Access Help	Opens the Office Assistant; type a question to open the entire Microsoft Access Help manual in a separate window in which you can search for information by the table of contents, index, or keyword
Show the Office Assistant	Presents the Office Assistant, an automated character that provides tips and interactive prompts while you are working
Hide the Office Assistant	Temporarily closes the Office Assistant for the working session
What's This	Changes the mouse pointer to �?; this special mouse pointer provides a short explanation of the icon or menu option that you click
Office on the Web	If you are connected to the Web, provides additional Microsoft information and support articles; this Web-based information is updated daily
Detect and Repair	Analyzes a database for possible data corruption and attempts to repair problems
About Microsoft Access	Provides the version and product ID of Access

Practice

► Concepts Review

Label each element of the Access window shown in Figure A-18.

FIGURE A-18

Match each term with the statement that describes it.

7. **Objects**

8. **Table**

9. **Record**

10. **Field**

11. **Datasheet**

a. A group of related fields, such as all the demographic information for one customer

b. A collection of records for a single subject, such as all the customer records

c. A category of information in a table, such as a customer's name, city, or state

d. A spreadsheet-like grid that displays fields as columns and records as rows

e. Seven types of these are contained in an Access database and are used to enter, enhance, and use the data within the database

Select the best answer from the list of choices.

12. **Which of the following is NOT a typical benefit of relational databases?**

a. Easier data entry

b. Faster information retrieval

c. Minimized duplicate data entry

d. Automatic trend analysis

13. Which of the following is NOT an advantage of managing data with a relational database versus a spreadsheet?

a. Doesn't require preplanning before data is entered   c. Provides greater security

b. Allows links between lists of information   d. Allows multiple users to enter data simultaneously

14. The object that holds all of the data within an Access database

a. Query   c. Form

b. Table   d. Report

15. The object that provides an easy-to-use data entry screen

a. Table   c. Form

b. Query   d. Report

16. This displays messages regarding the current database operation

a. Status bar   c. Database toolbar

b. Title bar   d. Object tabs

▶ Skills Review

1. Define database software.

a. Identify five disadvantages of using a paper system, such as index cards, to organize database information. Write down your answers to this and the following questions using complete sentences.

b. Identify five advantages of managing database information in Access versus using a spreadsheet product like Excel.

2. Learn database terminology.

a. Explain the relationship between a field, a record, a table, and a database.

b. Identify the seven objects of an Access database, and explain the main purpose of each.

c. Which object of an Access database is most important? Why?

3. Start Access and open a database.

a. Click the Start button, point to Programs, then click Microsoft Access.

b. Insert your Project Disk into the appropriate disk drive, click the Open an existing file option button, click More Files, then click OK.

c. In the Open dialog box, choose the correct drive, then open the Recycle-A database file.

d. Identify the following items. (*Hint*: To create a printout of this screen, press [Print Screen] to capture an image of the screen to the Windows clipboard, start any word-processing program, then click the Paste button. Print the document that now contains a picture of this screen, and identify the elements on the printout.)

- Database toolbar
- Recycle-A database window
- Menu bar
- Object buttons
- Objects bar
- Status bar

4. View the database window.

a. Maximize both the Access window and the Recycle-A Database window.

b. Click each of the objects, then write down the object names of each type that exist in the Recycle-A database.

- Tables
- Queries
- Reports
- Pages
- Macros
- Modules
- Forms

5. Navigate records.

a. Open the Clubs table.

b. Press [Tab] or [Enter] to move through the fields of the first record.

c. Press [Ctrl][End] to move to the last field of the last record.

d. Press [Ctrl][Home] to move to the first field of the first record.

e. Click the Last Record navigation button to quickly move to the Oak Hill Patriots record.

6. Enter records.

a. In the Clubs table, click the New Record button, then add the following records:

Name	Street	City	State	Zip	Phone	Leader	Club Number
EBC Angels	10100 Metcalf	Overland Park	KS	66001	555-7711	Michael Garrett	8
MOT Friends	111 Holmes	Kansas City	MO	65001	555-8811	Aaron Goldstein	9

b. Move the Club Number field from the last column of the datasheet to the first column.

7. Edit records.

a. Change the Name field in the first record from "Jaycees" to "JC Club."

b. Change the Name field in the second record from "Boy Scouts #1" to "Oxford Cub Scouts."

c. Change the Leader field in the fifth record from "Melanie Perry" to "Melanie Griffiths."

d. Enter your name and personal information (make up a club name) as a new record, and enter 99 as the Club Number.

e. Delete the record for Club Number 8.

8. Preview and print a datasheet.

a. Preview the Clubs table datasheet.

b. Use the Page Setup option on the File menu to change the page orientation from portrait to landscape.

c. Print the Clubs table datasheet.

9. Get Help and exit Access.

a. Close the Clubs table object, saving the changes.

b. Close the Recycle-A database.

c. Use Office Assistant to learn more about creating a database.

d. Exit Access.

▶ Independent Challenges

1. Ten examples of databases are given below. For each example, write a brief answer for the following.

a. What field names would you expect to find in this database?

b. Provide an example of two possible records for each database.

- Telephone directory
- College course offerings
- Restaurant menu
- Cookbook
- Movie listing
- Encyclopedia
- Shopping catalog
- Corporate inventory
- Party guest list
- Members of the House of Representatives

2. You are working with several civic groups in your area to coordinate a community-wide cleanup effort. You have started a database called "Recycle-A" that tracks the clubs, their trash deposits, and the trash centers that are participating in this effort. To complete this independent challenge:

a. Start Access.

b. Open the Recycle-A database from your Project Disk, and determine the number of objects of each type that exist in the database:

- Tables
- Queries
- Reports
- Pages
- Macros
- Modules
- Forms

c. Open the Deposits table, and answer the following questions:
  - How many fields does the table have?
  - How many records are there in the table?

d. Close the table, then exit Access.

3. You are working with several civic groups in your area to coordinate a community-wide cleanup effort. You have started a database called "Recycle-A" that tracks the clubs, their trash deposits, and the trash centers that are participating in this effort.

To complete this independent challenge:

a. Start Access and open the Recycle-A database from your Project Disk.

b. Add the following records to the Clubs table:

Club Number	Name	Street	City	State	Zip	Phone	Leader
10	Take Pride	222 Switzer St.	Olathe	KS	66001	555-2211	David Reis
11	Cub Scouts #321	333 Ward Pkwy.	Kansas City	MO	65002	555-8811	Daniel Langguth

c. Edit the following records in the Clubs table. The Street field has changed for Club Number 6 and the Phone and Leader fields have changed for Club Number 7.

Club Number	Name	Street	City	State	Zip	Phone	Leader
6	Girl Scouts #1	55 Oak Terrace	Shawnee	KS	68777	555-4444	Jonathan Bacon
7	Oak Hill Patriots	888 Switzer	Overland Park	KS	66444	555-9988	Cynthia Ralston

d. If you haven't already, add your name and personal information (make up a club name) and enter 99 as the Club Number. Print the datasheet.

e. Close the table, close the database, then exit Access.

4. The World Wide Web can be used to collect or research information that is used in corporate databases. MediaLoft often uses their intranet for this purpose. An intranet is a group of connected networks owned by a company or organization that is used for internal purposes. Intranets use internet software to handle the data communications, such as e-mail and Web pages, within an organization. These pages often provide company-wide information. MediaLoft has developed a Web page on the intranet that provides information about their products and customers. Eventually, MediaLoft will tie these Web pages directly to their database so that the information is dynamically tied to their working database. In this exercise, you'll retrieve the new customer information recorded on the intranet Web page, and enter it directly into the MediaLoft-A database.

To complete this independent challenge:

a. Connect to the Internet, and use your browser to go to the Medialoft intranet site at http://www.course.com/illustrated/MediaLoft/

b. Click the link for Our Customers.

c. Print the page that shows the information for the two new customers.

d. Disconnect from the Internet.

e. Start Access and open the MediaLoft-A database.

f. Open the Customers table.

g. Add the new customers to the table. They will become records 30 and 31. Add your name to the table with your personal information as record 32.

h. Review your work, print the datasheet, close the MediaLoft A-database, then exit Access.

Visual Workshop

Open the Recycle-A database on your Project Disk. Modify the existing Centers table, and enter a new record using your name as the contact and Center Number 99. The Street field for the first record has changed, the Hazardous field for the first two records has changed, and two new records have been added to the datasheet. See Figure A-19. Print the datasheet.

FIGURE A-19

	Center Number	Name	Street	City	State	Zip	Phone	Contact	Hazard
	1	Trash 'R Us	989 Main	Lenexa	KS	61111	555-7777	Ben Cartwright	☐
	2	You Deliver	12345 College	Overland Park	KS	63444	555-2222	Jerry Magliano	☐
	3	County Landfill	12444 Pflumm	Lenexa	KS	64222	555-4422	Jerry Lewis	☐
	4	Cans and Stuff	543 Holmes	Kansas City	MO	60011	555-2347	Julee Burton	☑
	5	We Love Trash	589 Switzer	Kansas City	KS	60022	555-3456	Doug Morrison	☑
*									☐

Centers : Table

Record: 1 of 5

Using
Tables and Queries

Objectives

MOUS ► **Plan a database**
MOUS ► **Create a table**
MOUS ► **Use Table Design view**
MOUS ► **Format a datasheet**
MOUS ► **Understand sorting, filtering, and finding**
MOUS ► **Sort records and find data**
MOUS ► **Filter records**
MOUS ► **Create a query**
MOUS ► **Use Query Design view**

Now that you are familiar with some of the basic Access terminology and features, you are ready to plan and build your own database. Your first task is to create the tables that store the data. Once the tables are created and the data is entered, you can use several techniques for finding specific information in the database, including sorting, filtering, and building queries. ◢▬ John Kim wants to build and maintain a database containing information about MediaLoft's products. The information in the database will be useful when John provides information for future sales promotions.

Planning a Database

The first and most important object in a database is the table object because it contains the **raw data**, the individual pieces of information stored in individual fields in the database. When you design a table, you identify the fields of information the table will contain and the type of data to be stored in each field. Some databases contain multiple tables linked together. John plans his database containing information about MediaLoft's products.

In planning a database it is important to:

Determine the purpose of the database and give it a meaningful name
The database will store information about MediaLoft's music products. You decide to name the database "MediaLoft," and name the first table "Music Inventory."

Determine what reports you want the database to produce
You want to be able to print inventory reports that list the products by artist, type of product (CD or cassette), quantity in stock, and price. These pieces of information will become the fields in the Music Inventory table.

Collect the raw data that will be stored in the database
The raw data for MediaLoft's products might be stored on index cards, in paper reports, and in other electronic formats, such as word-processed documents and spreadsheets. You can use Access to import data from many other electronic sources, which greatly increases your data entry efficiency.

Sketch the structure of each table, including field names and data types
Using the data you collected, identify the field name and data type for each field in each table as shown in Figure B-1. The **data type** determines what type of information you can enter in a field. For example, a field with a Currency data type does accept text. Properly defining the data type for each field helps you maintain data consistency and accuracy. Table B-1 lists the data types available within Access.

Choosing between the text and number data type

When assigning data types, you should avoid choosing "number" for a telephone or zip code field. Although these fields generally contain numbers, they should still be text data types. Consider the following: You may want to enter 1-800-BUY-BOOK in a telephone number field. This would not be possible if the field were designated as a number data type. When you sort the fields, you'll want them to sort alphabetically, like text fields. Consider the following zip codes: 60011 and 50011-8888. If the zip code field were designated as a number data type, the zip codes would be interpreted incorrectly as the values 60,011 and 500,118,888; and sort in that order, too.

FIGURE B-1: Music Inventory table field names and data types

Field Name	Data Type
RecordingID	AutoNumber
RecordingTitle	Text
RecordingArtist	Text
MusicCategory	Text
RecordingLabel	Text
Format	Text
NumberofTracks	Number
PurchasePrice	Currency
RetailPrice	Currency
Notes	Memo

TABLE B-1: Data types

data type	description of data	size
Text	Text information or combinations of text and numbers, such as a street address, name, or phone number	Up to 255 characters
Memo	Lengthy text such as comments or notes	Up to 64,000 characters
Number	Numeric information used in calculations, such as quantities	Several sizes available to store numbers with varying degrees of precision
Date/Time	Dates and times	Size controlled by Access to accommodate dates and times across thousands of years (for example, 1/1/1850 and 1/1/2150 are valid dates)
Currency	Monetary values	Size controlled by Access; accommodates up to 15 digits to the left of the decimal point and 4 digits to the right
AutoNumber	Integers assigned by Access to sequentially order each record added to a table	Size controlled by Access
Yes/No	Only one of two values stored (Yes/No, On/Off, True/False)	Size controlled by Access
OLE Object	Pointers stored that link files created in other programs, such as pictures, sound clips, documents, or spreadsheets	Up to one gigabyte
Hyperlink	Web addresses	Size controlled by Access
Lookup Wizard	Invokes a wizard that helps link the current table to another table (the final data type of the field is determined by choices made in the wizard; a field created with the lookup data type will display data from another table)	Size controlled through the choices made in the Lookup Wizard

Access 2000

Creating a Table

After you plan the structure of the database, your next step is to create the database file itself, which will eventually contain all of the objects such as tables, queries, forms, and reports. When you create a database, first you name it, and then you can build the first table object and enter data. Access offers several methods for creating a table. For example, you can import a table from another data source such as a spreadsheet, or use the Access **Table Wizard**, which provides interactive help to create the field names and data types for each field. John is ready to create the MediaLoft database. He uses the Table Wizard to create the Music Inventory table.

Steps 1 2 3 4

1. Start Access, click the **Blank Access database option button** in the Microsoft Access dialog box, then click **OK**
   The File New Database dialog box opens.

2. Type **MediaLoft** in the File name text box, insert your Project Disk in the appropriate drive, click the **Save in list arrow**, click the **drive**, then click **Create**
   The MediaLoft database file is created and saved on your Project Disk. The Table Wizard offers an efficient way to plan the fields of a new table.

3. If the Office Assistant appears on your screen, click **Help** on the menu bar, click **Hide the Office Assistant**, then double-click **Create table by using wizard** in the MediaLoft Database window
   The Table Wizard dialog box opens, as shown in Figure B-2. The Table Wizard offers 25 business and 20 personal sample tables from which you can select sample fields. The Recordings sample table, which is in the Personal category of tables, most closely matches the fields you want to include in the Music Inventory table.

4. Click the **Personal option button**, scroll down and click **Recordings** in the Sample Tables list box, then click the **Select All Fields button** >>
   Your Table Wizard dialog box should look like Figure B-3. At this point, you can change the suggested field names to better match your database.

5. Click **RecordingArtistID** in the Fields in my new table list box, click **Rename Field**, type **RecordingArtist** in the Rename field text box, then click **OK**

6. Click **Next**
   The second Table Wizard dialog box allows you to name the table and determine if Access sets the **primary key field**, a field that contains unique information for each record.

Trouble?

If you don't see all the fields in the table, it is because you have different settings on your monitor. Maximize the window to see all the fields, if necessary.

7. Type **Music Inventory**, make sure the **Yes, set a primary key for me option button** is selected, click **Next**, click the **Modify the table design option button**, then click **Finish**
   The table opens in **Design view**, shown in Figure B-4, which allows you to add, delete, or modify the fields in the table. The primary **key field symbol** indicates that the RecordingID field has been designated as the primary key field.

FIGURE B-2: Table Wizard

Business and personal categories

Sample tables

Sample fields for the selected table

Select All Fields button

FIGURE B-3: Table Wizard with Recordings table fields

Personal category chosen

Recordings table chosen

RecordingArtistID field

FIGURE B-4: Music Inventory table in Design view

View button

Key field symbol

Field names

Access 2000

Using Table Design View

Each database object has a **Design view** in which you can modify its structure. The Design view of a table allows you to add or delete fields, add **field descriptions**, or change other field properties. **Field properties** are additional characteristics of a field such as its size or default value. Using the Table Wizard, John was able to create a Music Inventory table very quickly. Now in Design view he modifies the fields to meet his needs. MediaLoft doesn't track purchase dates or release dates, but it does need to store retail price information in the database.

Steps

1. In the Music Inventory table's Design view, click **DatePurchased** in the Field Name column, click the **Delete Rows button** on the Table Design toolbar, click the **Year Released row selector**, click to delete the field, click the **Notes** field, then click the **Insert Rows button**

   The Year Released and Date Purchased fields are deleted from the table and a new row appears in which you can add the new field name.

2. Type **RetailPrice**, press **[Tab]**, type **C** (for Currency data type), then press **[Enter]**

   The new field is added to the Music Inventory table, as shown in Figure B-5. The data type of both the RecordingArtist and MusicCategoryID fields should be Text so that descriptive words can be entered in these fields rather than just numbers.

3. Click the **Number** data type in the RecordingArtist field, click the **Data Type list arrow**, click **Text**, click the **Number** data type in the MusicCategoryID field, click the **Data Type list arrow**, then click **Text**

   You must work in the table's Design view to make structural changes to the table.

4. Click to the right of **MusicCategoryID**, press **[Backspace]** twice, then click the **Save button** on the Table Design toolbar

   A description identifies a field and can list the types of data in that field.

5. Click the **MusicCategory Description cell**, then type **classical, country, folk, gospel, jazz, new age, rap, or rock**

   The **field size property** limits the number of characters allowed for each field.

6. Make sure the **MusicCategory** field is still selected, double-click **50** in the Field Size cell, then type **9**

   The longest entry in the MusicCategory field, "classical," is only nine characters. The finished Music Inventory table Design view should look like Figure B-6.

7. Click the **Datasheet View button** on the Table Design toolbar, click **Yes** to save the table, then type the following record into the new datasheet:

in field:	type:	in field:	type:
Recording ID	**[Tab]**	Format	**CD**
Recording Title	**No Words**	Number of Tracks	**12**
RecordingArtist	**Brickman, Jim**	Purchase Price	**$10.00**
Music Category ID	**New Age**	RetailPrice	**$13.00**
Recording Label	**Windham Hill**	Notes	

   You are finished working with the MediaLoft database for now.

8. Close the Music Inventory table, then close the MediaLoft database

   Data is saved automatically, so you were not prompted to save the record when you closed the datasheet.

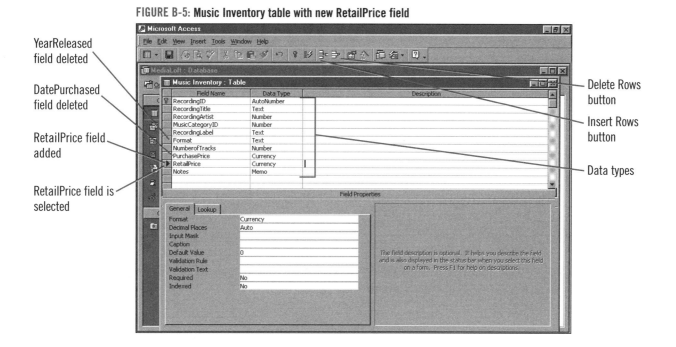

FIGURE B-5: Music Inventory table with new RetailPrice field

YearReleased field deleted

DatePurchased field deleted

RetailPrice field added

RetailPrice field is selected

Delete Rows button

Insert Rows button

Data types

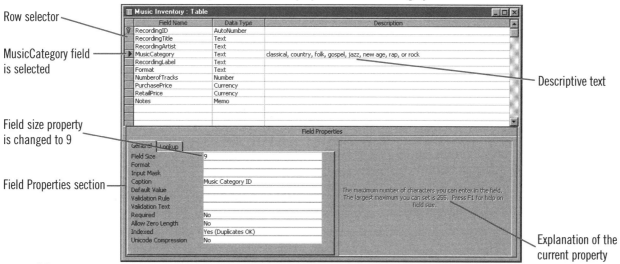

FIGURE B-6: Description and field size properties for MusicCategory field

Row selector

MusicCategory field is selected

Field size property is changed to 9

Field Properties section

Descriptive text

Explanation of the current property

CLUES TO USE

Learning about field properties

The properties of a field are the characteristics that define the field. Two properties are required for every field: Field Name and Data Type. Many other properties, such as Field Size, Format (the way the field is displayed on the datasheet), Caption, and Default Value, are defined in the Field Properties section of the table's Design view. As you add more property entries, you are generally restricting the amount or type of data that can be entered in the field, which also increases data entry accuracy. For example, you might change the Field Size property for a State field from the default value of 50 to 2 to eliminate an incorrect

entry such as "NYY." The available field properties change depending on the data type of the selected field. For example, there is no Field Size property for a Birth Date field, because Access controls the size of fields with a Date/Time data type. Database designers often insist on field names without spaces because they are easier to reference in other Access objects. The **Caption property**, however, can be used to override the technical field name with an easy-to-read Caption entry when the field name is displayed on datasheets, forms, and reports. When you create a table using the wizard, many fields have Caption properties.

Formatting a Datasheet

Even though the report object is the primary tool to create professional hard copy output from an Access database, you can print a datasheet too. Although you cannot create fancy headings or insert graphic images on a datasheet, you can change the fonts and colors as well as change the gridlines to dramatically change its appearance. John has been busy entering MediaLoft's music information in the Music Inventory table (which is stored in the MediaLoft-B database). He has also simplified many of the field names. Now he will print the Music Inventory datasheet using new fonts and colors.

Steps

1. Click the **Open button** on the Database toolbar, select the **MediaLoft-B** database from your Project Disk, then click **Open**
   The Music Inventory table has data that was entered by John Kim.

2. Click **Music Inventory** in the Tables Object window, then click the **Open button**
   Access displays the Music Inventory table, containing 58 records, as shown in Figure B-7. You can change the font and color of the datasheet to enhance its appearance.

3. Click **Format** on the menu bar, click **Font**, click **Comic Sans MS** in the Font list, then click **OK**
   Comic Sans MS is an informal font used for personal correspondence or internal memos. It simulates handwritten text, but is still very readable. You can also change the color and format of the datasheet gridlines.

4. Click **Format** on the menu bar, click **Datasheet**, click the **Gridline Color list arrow**, then click **Red**
   The Sample box in the Datasheet Formatting dialog box displays both the vertical and horizontal gridlines as red.

5. Click the **Border list arrow**, click **Vertical Gridline**, click the **Line Styles list arrow**, click **Transparent Border**, as shown in Figure B-8, then click **OK**
   You removed the vertical gridlines separating the fields. You can also change the left and right margins, and change the page orientation from portrait to landscape to fit all the fields across the page.

6. Click **File** on the menu bar, click **Page Setup**, double-click **1"** in the Top text box, type **0.75**, press **[Tab]**, type **0.75** in the Bottom text box, press **[Tab]**, type **0.75** in the Left text box, press **[Tab]**, type **0.75** in the Right text box, click the **Page tab**, click the **Landscape option button**, then click **OK**
   Print Preview displays your formatted datasheet as it will look when printed.

7. Click the **Print Preview button** on the Table Datasheet toolbar to preview the finished product, as shown in Figure B-9
   The red gridlines seem a bit too intense for your printout.

8. Click the **Close button** on the Print Preview toolbar, click **Format** on the menu bar, click **Datasheet**, click the **Gridline Color list arrow**, click **Silver**, then click **OK**
   Silver is the default gridline color.

FIGURE B-7: Music Inventory table datasheet

FIGURE B-8: Datasheet Formatting dialog box

Gridline Color
list arrow

Border list arrow

Line Styles list arrow

FIGURE B-9: Previewing the formatted datasheet

Understanding Sorting, Filtering, and Finding

The records of a datasheet are automatically sorted according to the data in the primary key field. Often, however, you'll want to view or print records in an entirely different sort order. Or you may want to display a subset of the records, such as those within the same music category or those below a certain retail price. Access makes it easy to sort, find data, and filter a datasheet with buttons on the Table Datasheet toolbar, summarized in Table B-2. John studies the sort, find, and filter features to learn how to find and retrieve information in his database.

Details

 Sorting refers to reorganizing the records in either ascending or descending order based on the contents of a field. Text fields sort from A to Z, number fields from the lowest to the highest value, and date/time fields from the oldest date to the date furthest into the future. In Figure B-10 the Music Inventory table has been sorted in ascending order on the Artist field. Notice that numbers sort before letters in an ascending sort order.

 Filtering means temporarily isolating a subset of records, as shown in Figure B-11. This is particularly useful because the subset can be formatted and printed just like the entire datasheet. You can produce a listing of all rock music or a listing based on any category, artist, or field in the datasheet. To remove a filter, click the Remove Filter button to view all the records in the datasheet.

 Finding refers to locating a specific piece of data, such as "Amy" or "500," within a field or an entire datasheet, similar to finding text in a word-processing document. The Find and Replace dialog box is shown in Figure B-12. The options in this dialog box are summarized below.

- **Find What:** Provides a text box for your search criteria. For example, you might want to find the text "Amy", "Beatles", or "Capitol Records" in the datasheet.

- **Look In:** Determines whether Access looks for the search criteria in the current field (in this case the Artist field) or in all fields.

- **Match:** Determines whether the search criteria must match the whole field's contents exactly, any part of the field, or the start of the field.

- **More:** Provides more options to limit your search. For example, it allows you to make your search criteria uppercase- or lowercase-sensitive.

- **Replace tab:** Provides a text box for you to specify "replacement text." In other words, you might want to search for every occurrence of "Compact Disc" and replace it with "CD" by entering "Compact Disc" as your search criteria and "CD" as your replacement text.

TABLE B-2: Sort, Filter, and Find buttons

name	button	purpose
Sort Ascending		Sorts records based on the selected field in ascending order (0 to 9, A to Z)
Sort Descending		Sorts records based on the selected field in descending order (Z to A, 9 to 0)
Filter By Selection		Filters records based on selected data and hides records that do not match
Filter By Form		Filters records based on more than one selection criteria by using the Filter By Form window
Apply Filter or Remove Filter		Applies or removes the filter
Find		Searches for a string of characters in the current field or all fields

FIGURE B-10: **Records sorted in ascending order by Artist**

Records sorted in ascending order by Artist

FIGURE B-11: **Records filtered by "Rock" category**

Sort Ascending button

Sort Descending button

Number of records in filtered subset

Apply Filter or Remove Filter button

Filter By Selection button

Selection criteria so only Records in Rock category display

FIGURE B-12: **Find and Replace dialog box**

Using wildcards in Find

Wildcards are symbols you can use as substitutes for characters to find information that matches your find criteria. Access uses these wildcards: the asterisk (*) represents any group of characters, the question mark (?) stands for any single character, and the pound sign (#) stands for a single number digit. For example, to find any word beginning with "S," type "s*" in the Find What text box.

Sorting Records and Finding Data

Sorting records and quickly finding information in a database are two powerful tools that help you work more efficiently. John needs to create several different printouts of the Music Inventory datasheet to satisfy various departments. The Marketing department wants a printout of records sorted by title and artist. The Accounting department wants a printout of records sorted from highest retail price to lowest.

Steps

1. **In the Music Inventory datasheet, click any cell in the Title field, then click the Sort Ascending button on the Table Datasheet toolbar**
   The records are listed in an A-to-Z sequence based on the data in the Title field, as shown in Figure B-13. Next you'll sort the records according to artist.

2. **Click any cell in the Artist field, then click**
   The table is sorted alphabetically in ascending order by Artist. You can preview and print a sorted datasheet at any time.

QuickTip
Scroll to the right if necessary to see this field.

3. **Click any cell in the Retail field, then click the Sort Descending button on the Table Datasheet toolbar**
   The records are sorted in descending order on the value in the Retail field. The CD that sells for the highest retail price, "Skyline Firedance," is listed as the first record. To put the records back in their original order, you can click the key field, RecordingID, and click the Sort Ascending button. Access also lets you find all records based on any search word.

4. **Click any cell in the Title field, then click the Find button on the Table Datasheet toolbar**
   The Find and Replace dialog box opens. You know MediaLoft will want to find the titles that are going to be hot sellers during the Christmas season.

5. **Type Christmas in the Find What text box, click the Match list arrow, then click Any Part of Field, as shown in Figure B-14**
   Access will find all occurrences of the word "Christmas" in the Title field, whether it is the first, middle, or last part of the title. "Christmas" is the search criteria.

6. **Click Find Next, then if necessary drag the Find and Replace dialog box up and to the right to better view the datasheet**
   If you started the search at the top of the datasheet, "A Family Christmas" is the first title found. You can look for more occurrences of "Christmas."

7. **Click Find Next to find the next occurrence of the word "Christmas," then click Find Next as many times as it takes to move through all the records**
   When no more occurrences of the search criteria "Christmas" are found, Access lets you know that no more matching records can be found.

8. **Click OK when prompted that Access has finished searching the records, then click Cancel to close the Find and Replace dialog box**

RecordingID	Title	Artist	Category	Label	Format	Tracks
55	A Christmas Album	Grant, Amy	Folk	Reunion Records	CD	11
46	A Family Christmas	Tesh, John	New Age	GTS Records	CD	14
32	A Winter's Solstice	Windham Hill Artists	New Age	Windham	CD	10
53	Abbey Road	Beatles, The	Rock	Capitol Records	Vinyl	14
22	Autumn	Winston, George	New Age	Windham	Vinyl	7
51	Blue	Mitchell, Joni	Rock	Liberty Records	CD	10
16	Can We Go Home Now	Roches, The	Folk	Ryko	CD	11
35	Christmas	Mannheim Steamroller	New Age	Sony Music	CD	11
28	Christmas to Christmas	Greenwood, Lee	Country	MCA Records	CD	10
31	Closeup	Sandborn, David	Jazz	MCA Records	Cassette	10
2	Come Walk With Me	Adams, Oleta	Gospel	CBS Records	CD	10
54	Cosmic Thing	B-52s	Rock	Warner Records	CD	10
37	Cracked Rear View	Hootie and the Blowfi	Rock	Arista	CD	11
13	Daydream	Carey, Mariah	Rock	Columbia	CD	12
52	Decade	Young, Neil	Rock	A&M Records	CD	10
20	December	Winston, George	New Age	Windham	CD	12
26	Fantasia	Stokowski, Leopold	Classical	Buena Vista Records	CD	6
40	Favorite Overtures	Bernstein, Leonard	Classical	CBS Records	Vinyl	5
39	Foreign Affair	Turner, Tina	Rock	Capitol Records	Vinyl	12
43	Garth Brooks Live	Brooks, Garth	Country	Liberty Records	CD	10

Record: 1 of 58

Records are sorted in
ascending order by Title

FIGURE B-14: Specify "Christmas" as the search criteria in the Title field

Field you are
searching

Find and Replace

Find | Replace

Find What: Christmas

Find Next
Cancel

Look In: Title

Match: Any Part of Field

More >>

Tells Access to find the search
criteria anywhere in the selected field

CLUES TO USE

Sorting on more than one field

The telephone book sorts records by last name (**primary sort field**) and when ties occur on the last name (for example, two "Smiths"), it further sorts the records by first name (**secondary sort field**). Access allows you to sort by more than one field using the query object, which you will learn more about later in this unit. Queries allow you to specify more than one sort field in Query Design view, evaluating the sort orders from left to right (the leftmost sort field is the primary sort field).

Filtering Records

Sorting allows you to reorder all the records of a datasheet. Filtering the datasheet displays only those records that match criteria. **Criteria** are rules or limiting conditions you set. For example, you may want to show only those records where the Category field is equal to "Rap," or where the PurchasePrice field is less than $10. Once you have filtered a datasheet to display a subset of records, you can still sort the records and find data just as if you were working with the entire datasheet. To make sure the Filter By Form grid is clear of any previous entries, you should click the Clear Grid button [X]. The Accounting department asked John for a printout of cassettes with a retail price of $15 or more. John uses the datasheet's filter buttons to answer this request.

Steps

1. **In the Music Inventory datasheet, click the RecordingID field, click the Sort Ascending button** [button icon] **on the Table Datasheet toolbar, click any occurrence of Cassette in the Format field, then click the Filter By Selection button** [icon] **on the Table Datasheet toolbar**
Twelve records are selected, as shown in Figure B-15. Filter By Selection is a fast and easy way to filter the records for an exact match (that is, where Format field value is *equal to* Cassette). To filter for comparative data and to specify more complex criteria (for example, where PurchasePrice is *equal to* or *greater than* $15), you must use the Filter By Form feature. See Table B-3 for more information on comparison operators.

QuickTip
If you click the Field List arrow, you can pick an entry from a list of existing entries in that field.

2. **Click the Filter By Form button** [icon] **on the Table Datasheet toolbar, click the Retail field, then type >=15**
The finished Filter By Form window is shown in Figure B-16. The previous Filter By Selection criteria, "Cassette" in the Format field, is still valid in the grid. Access distinguishes between text and numeric entries by placing quotation marks around text entries. You can widen a column to display the entire criteria. Filter By Form is more powerful than Filter By Selection because it allows you to use comparison operators such as >=. Filter By Form also allows you to enter criteria for more than one field at a time where *both* criteria must be "true" in order for the record to be shown in the resulting datasheet.

3. **Click the Apply Filter button** [icon] **on the Filter/Sort toolbar, then scroll to the right to display the Retail field**
Only two records are true for both criteria, as shown in Figure B-17. The Record Navigation buttons in the lower-left corner of the datasheet display how many records are in the filtered subset. You can remove the current filter to view all the records in the datasheet at any time by clicking the Remove Filter button.

4. **Click the Remove Filter button** [icon] **on the Table Datasheet toolbar**
Be sure to remove existing filters before you apply a new filter or you will end up filtering the existing subset of records versus the entire datasheet. Next find all selections produced under the "A&M Records" recording label.

5. **Click any cell in the Label field, click** [icon], **A&M Records is selected as the Label entry, then click** [icon]
Using both the sort and filter buttons, you quickly found the five records that met the "A&M Records" criteria.

6. **Close the datasheet, then click Yes if prompted to save the changes to the Music Inventory table**
Any filters applied to a datasheet will be removed the next time you open the datasheet, but the sort order will be saved.

FIGURE B-15: Music Inventory datasheet filtered for "Cassette" records

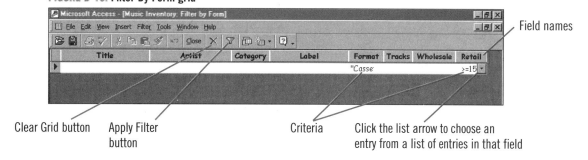

12 records are selected

All records have Cassette in Format field

FIGURE B-16: Filter By Form grid

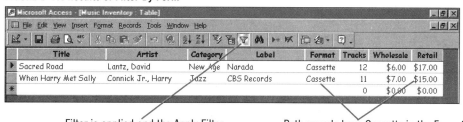

Field names

Clear Grid button   Apply Filter button

Criteria   Click the list arrow to choose an entry from a list of entries in that field

FIGURE B-17: Results of Filter By Form

Filter is applied and the Apply Filter button becomes the Remove Filter button

Both records have Cassette in the Format field and all records have a Retail value >=15

TABLE B-3: Comparison operators

operator	description	expression	meaning
>	Greater than	>500	Numbers greater than 500
>=	Greater than or equal to	>=500	Numbers greater than or equal to 500
<	Less than	<"Bunin"	Names from A through Bunim, but not Bunin
<=	Less than or equal to	<="Calloway"	Names from A through, and including, Calloway
<>	Not equal to	<>"Cyclone"	Any name except for Cyclone

Searching for blank fields

Is Null and **Is Not Null** are two other types of common criteria. Is Null criteria will find all records where no entry has been made in the field.

Is Not Null will find all records where there is any entry in the field, even if the entry is 0. Primary key fields cannot have a null entry.

Access 2000

Creating a Query

A **query** is a database object that creates a datasheet of specified fields and records from one or more tables. It displays the answer to a "question" about the data in your database. You can edit, navigate, sort, find, and filter a query's datasheet just like a table's datasheet. Because a query datasheet is a subset of data, however, it is similar to a filter, but much more powerful. One of the most important differences is that a query is a saved object within the database, which means that it does not need to be recreated each time you want to see that particular subset of data. A **filter** is a temporary view of the data whose criteria is discarded when you remove the filter or close the datasheet. Table B-4 compares the two. ✎──── John uses a query to correct data in the table and then find all of the music selections in the "country" category.

Steps 1234

1. Click **Queries** on the Objects bar, then double-click **Create query by using wizard**
The Simple Query Wizard dialog box opens, allowing you to choose the table or query which contains the fields you want to display in the query. You select the fields in the order you want them to appear on the query datasheet.

> **QuickTip**
> You also can double-click a field to move it from the Available Fields list to the Selected Fields list.

2. Click **Category** in the Available Fields list, click the **Select Single Field button** ⟩, click **Title**, click ⟩, click **Artist**, click ⟩, click **Tracks**, then click ⟩
The Simple Query Wizard dialog box should look like Figure B-18.

3. Click **Next**, click **Next** to accept the **Detail option** in the next dialog box, accept the title **Music Inventory Query**, make sure the **Open the query to view information option button** is selected, then click **Finish**
The query's datasheet opens, as shown in Figure B-19, with all 58 records, but with only the four fields that you requested in the query wizard. You can use a query datasheet to edit or add information.

> **QuickTip**
> The sort, filter, and find buttons work the same way whether you are working with a query or table datasheet.

4. Double-click **10** in the Tracks cell for record 7, "No Words", then type **11**
This record is now correct in the database.

5. Click the **Design View button** ⊠ on the Query Datasheet toolbar
The **Query Design view** opens, showing you a list of fields in the Music Inventory table in the upper portion of the window, and the fields you have requested for the query in the **query design grid** in the lower portion of the window.

6. Click the **Criteria cell** for the Category field, then type **country**, as shown in Figure B-20
Query Design view is the view in which you add, delete, or change the order of fields, sort the records, or add criteria to limit the number of records shown in the resulting datasheet. Any change made in Query Design view is saved with the query object.

7. Click the **Datasheet View button** ▦ on the Query Design toolbar
The resulting datasheet has four records that match the criteria "country" in the Category field. You can save a query with a name that accurately describes the resulting datasheet.

> **QuickTip**
> The only time you need to save changes in an Access database is when you make structural changes to an object in Design view.

8. Click **File** on the menu bar, click **Save As**, type **Country Music** in the Save Query 'Music Inventory Query' To text box, click **OK**, then close the query datasheet
Both the Music Inventory Query and Country Music queries are saved in this database as objects that you can access in the MediaLoft-B database window.

FIGURE B-18: **Simple Query Wizard dialog box**

The available fields
come from this
object

Select Single Field
button

Fields for this query

FIGURE B-19: **Music Inventory Query datasheet**

Design View button

Edit this entry

FIGURE B-20: **Query Design view**

Datasheet View
button

Music Inventory
field list

Criteria cell for
Category field with
country criteria

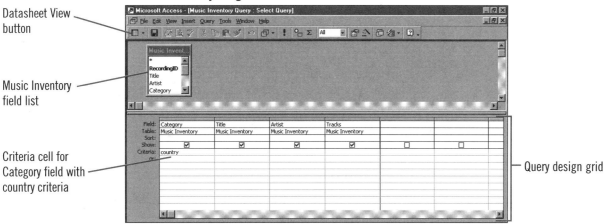

Query design grid

TABLE B-4: **Queries vs. filters**

characteristics	filters	queries
Are saved as an object in the database	No	Yes
Can be used to select a subset of records in a datasheet	Yes	Yes
Can be used to select a subset of fields in a datasheet	No	Yes
Its resulting datasheet can be used to enter and edit data	Yes	Yes
Its resulting datasheet can be used to sort, filter, and find records	Yes	Yes
Is commonly used as the source of data for a form or report	No	Yes
Can calculate sums, averages, counts, and other types of summary statistics across records	No	Yes
Can be used to create calculated fields	No	Yes

Using Query Design View

Every object in the database has a Design view in which you change the structure of the object. You can build a query by using the Query Design view directly or let the Query Wizard help you. In either case, if you want to add criteria to limit the number of records that you view in the datasheet, or if you want to change the fields you are viewing, you must use the query's Design view. ✏ John wants the Country Music query to also display the Retail field. In addition, he wants to add the folk music records and sort all the records according to the recording artist.

Steps 1234

1. Click the **Country Music query** in the MediaLoft-B Database window, click the **Design button** 🖾 in the database window, then click the **Restore button** 🗗 (if the window is maximized)

Query Design view opens, displaying the current fields and criteria for the Country Music query. To add fields to the query, you can drag the fields from the upper field list and place them in any order in the grid.

> **Trouble?**
>
> You may have to scroll through the Music Inventory field list to display the Retail field.

2. Click the **Retail field** in the Music Inventory field list, then drag the **Retail field** to the **Tracks Field cell** in the query design grid

The Query Design view now looks like Figure B-21. The Retail field is added to the query design grid between the Artist and Tracks fields. When you dropped the Retail field into the fourth column position of the query design grid, the Tracks field moved to the right to make room for the new field. You can also change the order of existing fields in the query design grid.

> **QuickTip**
>
> To remove fields from the query design grid, click the field selector, then press [Delete].

3. In the second column, click **Title**, click the **Title list arrow**, click **Artist**, click **Artist** in the third column, click the **Artist list arrow**, then click **Title**

You have switched the order of the Title and Artist fields. You can also move fields by dragging them left and right in the query design grid by clicking the field selector, and dragging the field to the new location. The query design grid also displays criteria that limit the number of records in the resulting datasheet.

4. Click the **or: criteria cell** under the "country" criteria of the Category field, then type **folk**

This additional criteria expression will add the folk selections to the current country selections. You also can enter Or criteria in one cell of the query design grid by entering "country" or "folk," but using two rows of the query design grid inherently joins the criteria in an Or expression.

5. Click the **Sort cell** for the Artist field, click the **Artist Sort list arrow**, then click **Ascending**

The final Query Design view, as shown in Figure B-22, will find all records that match the Category criteria for "country" or "folk" and sort the records in ascending order by Artist. Notice that text criteria in the query design grid are surrounded by quotation marks (as were filter criteria), but that you did not need to type these characters.

6. Click the **Datasheet view button** 🖩 on the Query Design toolbar

Eight records are displayed in both the country and folk music categories, sorted in ascending order by Artist, as shown in Figure B-23.

7. Click **File** on the menu bar, click **Save As**, type **Country and Folk**, click **OK**, then click the **Print button** 🖨 on the Query Datasheet toolbar

8. Close the query datasheet, close the MediaLoft-B database, then exit Access

Scroll bar for Music Inventory field list

FIGURE B-21: **Query Design view with new field, Retail**

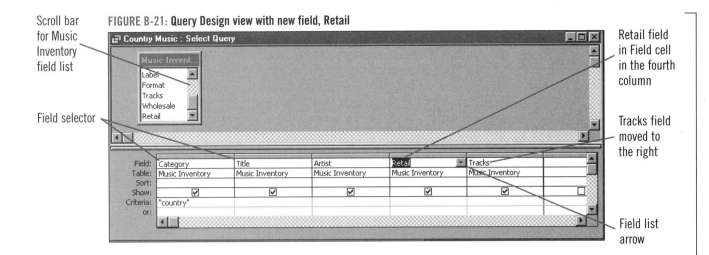

Field selector

Retail field in Field cell in the fourth column

Tracks field moved to the right

Field list arrow

Field order of Artist and Title fields is changed

FIGURE B-22: **Adding Or criteria and specifying a sort order**

Sort list arrow

Or criteria for the Category field

FIGURE B-23: **Final query datasheet**

Only Country or Folk records are displayed

Records are sorted in ascending order by Artist

Eight records are selected

Understanding And and Or criteria

Criteria placed on different rows of the query design grid are considered Or criteria. In other words, a record may be true for *either* row of criteria in order for it to be displayed on the resulting datasheet. Placing additional criteria in the *same* row, however, is considered the And criteria. For example, if "folk" were in the Category Criteria cell and >10 in the Retail Criteria cell, *both* criteria must be true in order for the record to be displayed in the resulting datasheet.

Practice

▶ Concepts Review

Label each element of the Select Query window shown in Figure B-24.

FIGURE B-24

Match each term with the statement that describes it.

8. **Primary key**
9. **Table Wizard**
10. **Filter**
11. **Data type**
12. **Query**

a. Determines what type of data can be stored in each field
b. Provides interactive help to create the field names and data types for each field
c. A database object that creates a datasheet of specified fields and records from one or more tables
d. A field that contains unique information for each record
e. Creates a temporary subset of records

Select the best answer from the list of choices.

13. Which data type would be best for a field that was going to store birth dates?
   a. Text
   b. Number
   c. AutoNumber
   d. Date/Time
14. Which data type would be best for a field that was going to store Web addresses?
   a. Text
   b. Memo
   c. OLE
   d. Hyperlink
15. Which data type would be best for a field that was going to store telephone numbers?
   a. Text
   b. Number
   c. OLE
   d. Hyperlink
16. Each of the following is true about a filter, *except*
   a. It creates a temporary datasheet of records that match criteria.
   b. The resulting datasheet can be sorted.
   c. The resulting datasheet includes all fields in the table.
   d. A filter is automatically saved as an object in the database.
17. Sorting refers to
   a. Reorganizing the records in either ascending or descending order.
   b. Selecting a subset of fields and/or records to view as a datasheet from one or more tables.
   c. Displaying only those records that meet certain criteria.
   d. Using Or and And criteria in the query design grid.

18. Which criteria would be used in a Category field to find all music except that in the rap category?
    a. /=/"rap"
    b. <>"rap"
    c. NULL "rap"
    d. IS NULL "rap"

 # Skills Review

1. **Plan a database.**
   a. Plan a database that will contain the names and addresses of physicians. You can use the local yellow pages to gather the information.
   b. On paper, sketch the Table Design view of a table that will hold this information. Write the field names in one column and the data types for each field in the second column.

2. **Create a table.**
   a. Start Access and use the Blank Access database option to create a database. Save the file as "Doctors" on your Project Disk.
   b. Use the Table Wizard to create a new table.
   c. Make sure the Business option button is selected. In the Sample Tables list, click Contacts.
   d. In the Sample Fields list box, choose each of the fields in the following order for your table: ContactID, FirstName, LastName, Address, City, StateOrProvince, PostalCode, Title.
   e. Rename the StateOrProvince field as "State."
   f. Name the table "Addresses," and allow Access to set the primary key field.
   g. Click the Modify the table design option button in the last Table Wizard dialog box, then click Finish.

3. **Use Table Design view.**
   a. In the first available blank row, add a new field called "PhoneNumber" with a Text data type.
   b. Change the Field Size property of the State field from 20 to 2.
   c. Insert a field named "Suite" with a Text data type between the Address and City fields.
   d. Add the description "M.D." or "D.O." to the Title field.
   e. Save and close the Addresses table, then close the Doctors database, but don't exit Access.

4. **Format a datasheet.**
   a. Open the Doctors-B database from your Project Disk. Open the Doctor Addresses table datasheet.
   b. Change the font to Arial Narrow, and the font size to 9.
   c. Change the gridline color to black, and change the vertical gridline to a transparent border.
   d. Change the page orientation to landscape and all of the margins to 0.5". Preview the datasheet (it should fit on one page), then print it.

5. **Understand sorting, filtering, and finding.**
   a. On a sheet of paper, identify three ways that you might want to sort an address list, such as the Doctor Addresses datasheet. Be sure to specify both the field you would sort on and the sort order (ascending or descending).
   b. On a sheet of paper, identify three ways that you might want to filter an address list, such as the Doctor Addresses datasheet. Be sure to specify both the field you would filter on and the criteria that you would use.

6. **Sort records and find data.**
   a. Sort the Doctor Addresses records in ascending order on the Last field, then list the first two doctors on paper.
   b. Sort the Doctor Addresses records in descending order on the Zip field, then list the first two doctors on paper.
   c. Find the records in which the Title field contains "D.O." How many records did you find?
   d. Find the records where the Zip field contains "64012." How many records did you find?

Access 2000

7. Filter records.

   a. In the Doctor Addresses datasheet, filter the records for all physicians with the Title "D.O."

   b. In the Doctor Addresses datasheet, filter the records for all physicians with the title "M.D." in the "64012" zip code, then print the datasheet.

8. Create a query.

   a. Use the Query Wizard to create a new query based on the Doctor Addresses table with the following fields: First, Last, City, State, Zip.

   b. Name the query "Doctors in Missouri," then view the datasheet.

   c. In Query Design view, add the criteria "MO" to the State field, then view the datasheet.

   d. Change Mark Garver's last name to Garvey.

9. Use Query Design view.

   a. Modify the Doctors in Missouri query to include only those doctors in Kansas City, Missouri. Be sure that the criteria is in the same row so that both criteria must be true for the record to be displayed.

   b. Save the query with the name "Doctors in Kansas City Missouri." Print the query results, then close the query datasheet.

   c. Modify the Doctors in Kansas City Missouri query so that the records are sorted in ascending order on the last name, and add "DoctorNumber" as the first field in the datasheet.

   d. Print and save the sorted query's datasheet, then close the datasheet.

   e. Close the Doctors-B database and exit Access.

▶ Independent Challenges

1. You want to start a database to track your personal video collection.
To complete this independent challenge:

   a. Start Access and create a new database called "Movies" on your Project Disk.

   b. Using the Table Wizard, create a table based on the Video Collection sample table in the personal category with the following fields: MovieTitle, YearReleased, Rating, Length, DateAcquired, PurchasePrice.

   c. Rename the YearReleased field as "Year" and the PurchasePrice field as "Price."

   d. Name the table "Video Collection," and allow Access to set a primary key field.

   e. Modify the Video Collection table in Design view with the following changes:

     • Change the Rating field size property to 4.

     • Change the Length field to a Number data type.

     • Change the DateAcquired field name to DatePurchased.

     • Add a field between Rating and Length called "PersonalRating" with a Number data type.

     • In the description of the PersonalRating field, type: My personal rating on a scale from 1 (bad) to 10 (great).

   f. Save and close the Video Collection table, and close the Movies database.

2. You work for a marketing company that sells medical supplies to doctors' offices.
To complete this independent challenge:

   a. Open the Doctors-B database on your Project Disk, then open the Doctors Addresses table datasheet.

   b. Filter the records to find all those physicians who live in Grandview, then print the filtered datasheet.

   c. Sort the records by last name, change the font size to 12, resize the columns so all the data within each column is visible, change the page orientation to landscape, then print the datasheet.

   d. Using the Query Wizard, create a query with the following fields: First, Last, Phone.

   e. Name the query "Telephone Query." Sort the records in ascending order by last name, then print the datasheet.

f. Add the Title field to the third field position, then delete the First field. Save and close the query.

g. Modify the Telephone Query so that the State field is added to the fourth field position. Add criteria so that only those physicians in Missouri are shown on the resulting datasheet.

h. Print, save, and close the query. Close the Doctors-B database, then exit Access.

3. You want to create a database to keep track of your personal contacts.
To complete this independent challenge:

a. Start Access and create a new database called "People" on your Project Disk.

b. Using the Table Wizard, create a table based on the Addresses sample table in the Personal category with the following fields: FirstName, LastName, SpouseName, Address, City, StateOrProvince, PostalCode, EmailAddress, HomePhone, Birthdate.

c. Name the table Contact Info, allow Access to set the primary key field, and choose the Enter data directly into the table option in the last Table Wizard dialog box.

d. Enter at least five records into the table, making sure that two people have the same last name. Use your name for one of the records. You do not have to enter real names and addresses into the other records.

e. Press [Tab] to move through the Contact InfoID field.

f. Sort the records in ascending order by last name.

g. Adjust the column widths, change the datasheet margins, change the paper orientation, and make other adjustments, as necessary, to print the five records on one page.

h. Using the Query Wizard, create a query with the following fields from the Contact Info table in this order: LastName, FirstName, Birthdate.

i. Name the query Birthday List, and in Query Design view, sort the records in ascending order by LastName and then by FirstName.

j. Save the query as Sorted Birthday List, then view the query.

k. Change the Birthdate field to 8/20/58 for one of the records in the query datasheet.

l. Print the query's datasheet, close the query, then close the People database and exit Access.

4. MediaLoft has developed a Web site that provides information about their products and allows viewers to vote for their favorite music collections. In this exercise, you will print the Web page from the MediaLoft intranet site that records the People's choice awards. Then you will enter that information in the database, and create a query that displays only the top records.

a. Connect to the Internet, and use your browser to go to the MediaLoft intranet site at http://www.course.com/illustrated/medialoft

b. Click the link for Products to go to the Web page summarizing the most popular music selection in several categories as determined by a recent vote of customers.

c. Print the People's Choice Web page, then disconnect from the Internet.

d. Open the MediaLoft-B database, and then open the Music Inventory table in Design view.

e. Add a field called PeoplesChoice at the end of the field list with a Yes/No data type.

f. Find the six records listed on the People's Choice Web page (*Hint*: Use the Find and Sort buttons). Then place a checkmark in the PeoplesChoice field in your database for the six records to indicate that they were contest winners.

g. Using the Query Wizard, create a query that is based on the Music Inventory table with the following fields: Category, Title, Artist, Retail, PeoplesChoice.

h. Show all the Detail records, name the query "Peoples Choice Query," then modify the query so that only those records with "Yes" in the PeoplesChoice field are displayed.

i. Save and print the Peoples Choice Query datasheet.

j. Close the Peoples Choice Query, close the MediaLoft-B database, then exit Access.

Open the MediaLoft-B database and create a query based on the Music Inventory table that displays the datasheet

▶ Visual Workshop

Open the MediaLoft-B database and create a query based on the Music Inventory table that displays the datasheet shown in Figure B-25. Notice that only the Jazz category is displayed and that the records are sorted in a descending order on the Retail field. Save the query as "Jazz Selections" in the MediaLoft-B database.

FIGURE B-25

Using
Forms

Objectives

- ► Plan a form
- MOUS ► Create a form
- MOUS ► Move and resize controls
- MOUS ► Modify labels
- MOUS ► Modify text boxes
- ► Modify tab order
- MOUS ► Enter and edit records
- MOUS ► Insert an image

A **form** is an Access database object that allows you to arrange the fields of a record in any layout. Although the datasheet view of a table or query can be used to navigate, edit, and enter new information, all of the fields for one record are sometimes not visible unless you scroll left or right. A form fixes that problem by using the screen to show the fields of only one record at a time. Forms are often the primary object used to enter, edit, and find data. ✎ More people are becoming excited about the MediaLoft music inventory database. They have asked John Kim to create a form to make it easier to access, enter, and update this important inventory data.

Planning a Form

Properly organized and well-designed forms make a tremendous difference in the productivity of the end user. Since forms are the primary object used to enter and edit data, time spent planning a form is time well spent. Forms are often built to match a **source document** (for example, an employment application or a medical history form) to facilitate fast and accurate data entry. Now, however, it is becoming more common to type data directly into the database rather than first recording it on paper. Form design considerations, such as clearly labeled fields and appropriate formatting, are important. Other considerations include how the user tabs from field to field, and what type of **control** is used to display the data. See Table C-1 for more information on form controls. 🖋️ John considers the following form design considerations when planning his Music Inventory form.

Details

 Determine the overall purpose of the form

Have a good understanding of what information you need to gather through the form. This purpose often becomes the form's title such as "Music Inventory Entry Form."

 Determine the underlying record source

The **record source** is either a table or query object, and contains the fields and records that the form will display.

 Gather the source documents used to design your form, or sketch the form by hand if a paper form does not exist

When sketching the form, be sure to list all the fields and instructions you want the form to display.

 Determine the best type of control to use for each element on the form

Figures C-1 and C-2 show examples of several controls. **Bound controls** display data from the underlying record source and are also used to edit and enter new data. **Unbound controls** do not change from record to record and exist only to clarify or enhance the appearance of the form.

TABLE C-1: Form Controls

name	used to:	bound or unbound
Label	Provide consistent descriptive text as you navigate from record to record	Unbound
Text box	Display, edit, or enter data for each record from an underlying record source	Bound
List box	Display a list of possible data entries	Bound
Combo box	Display a list of possible data entries for a field, and also provide text box for an entry from the keyboard; a "combination" of the list box and text box controls	Bound
Tab control	Create a three-dimensional aspect to a form so that controls can be organized and displayed by clicking the "tabs"	Unbound
Check box	Display "yes" or "no" answers for a field; if the box is "checked" it displays "yes" information	Bound
Toggle button	Display "yes" or "no" answers for a field; if the button is "pressed," it displays "yes" information	Bound
Option button	Display a limited list of possible choices for field	Bound
Bound image control	Display OLE data, such as a picture	Bound
Unbound image control	Display picture or clip art that doesn't change as you navigate from record to record	Unbound
Line and Rectangle controls	Draw lines and rectangles on the form	Unbound
Command button	Provide an easy way to initiate a command or run a macro	Unbound

FIGURE C-1: Sample Form Controls

Tab controls

Option group

Labels

List box

Combo box

Text boxes

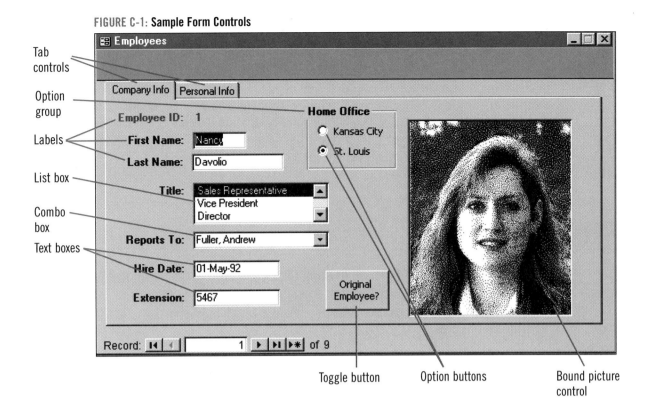

Toggle button   Option buttons   Bound picture control

FIGURE C-2: Sample Form Controls

Unbound image

Rectangle

Command buttons

Check box

Creating a Form

You can create a form from scratch using **Form Design view**, or you can use the **Form Wizard** to create an initial form object that can be modified later if needed. The Form Wizard provides options for selecting fields, an overall layout, a style, and a form title. John created a sketch and made some notes on how he'd like the final Music Inventory form arranged, shown in Figure C-3. He uses the Form Wizard to get started.

1. Start Access, click the **Open an existing file option button**, then open the **MediaLoft-C** database from your Project Disk

This MediaLoft-C database contains an enhanced Music Inventory table. John added more fields and records.

QuickTip

To hide the Office Assistant, click Help on the menu bar, then click Hide Office Assistant.

2. Click **Forms** on the Objects bar in the MediaLoft-C Database window, then double-click **Create form by using wizard**

The Music Inventory table includes all of the fields required in the Music Inventory form.

3. Click the **Select All Fields button** >> , click **Next**, click the **Columnar layout option button**, click **Next**, click the **Standard** style, click **Next**, then click **Finish** to accept the name **Music Inventory** for the form

The Music Inventory form opens in **Form view**, as shown in Figure C-4. Descriptive labels appear in the first column, and text boxes that display data from the underlying records appear in the second column. A check box control displays the yes/no data in the PeoplesChoice field. You can enter, edit, find, sort, and filter records using the form.

QuickTip

Sort, filter, and find buttons work the same way in a form as a datasheet, except that a form generally shows only one record at a time.

4. Click the **Artist text box**, click the **Sort Ascending button** on the Form View toolbar, then click the **Next Record button** to move to the second record

The "Adams, Oleta" record is second when the records are sorted in ascending order by recording artist.

5. Click the **Last Record button** on the Music Inventory form

Neil Young's "Decade" is the last record when the records are sorted in ascending order.

6. Click the **Close button** on the Music Inventory form title bar to close the form

The new Music Inventory form object appears in the Forms section of the MediaLoft-C Database window.

Using AutoForm

You can quickly create a form by clicking a table or query object in the database window, and then clicking the New Object:AutoForm button on the Database toolbar. AutoForm offers no prompts or dialog boxes; it instantly creates a form that displays all the fields in the previously chosen table or query using the same options as those you chose the last time you used the Form Wizard.

FIGURE C-3: Sketch of Music Inventory form

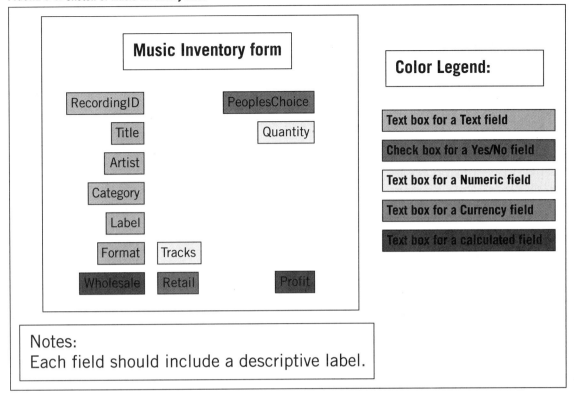

Music Inventory form

RecordingID

PeoplesChoice

Title

Quantity

Artist

Category

Label

Format   Tracks

Wholesale   Retail   Profit

Color Legend:

Text box for a Text field

Check box for a Yes/No field

Text box for a Numeric field

Text box for a Currency field

Text box for a calculated field

Notes:
Each field should include a descriptive label.

FIGURE C-4: Music Inventory form

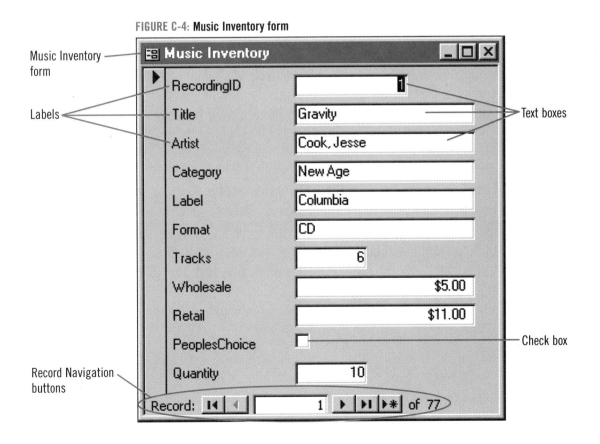

Music Inventory form

Labels

Record Navigation buttons

Text boxes

Check box

Access 2000

Access 2000

Moving and Resizing Controls

After you create a form, you can modify the size, location, and appearance of existing controls in Form Design view. Form Design view also allows you to add or delete controls. John moves and resizes the controls on the form to better match his original design.

Trouble?

Be sure you open the Design view of the Music Inventory form and not the Music Inventory table.

1. Click the **Music Inventory form**, click the **Design button** in the MediaLoft-C Database window, then click the **Maximize button** to maximize the Design view of the Music Inventory form

The Design view of the Music Inventory form opens. The **Toolbox toolbar** contains buttons that allow you to add controls to the form. The **field list** contains the fields in the underlying object. You can toggle both of these screen elements on and off as needed. Widening the form gives you more room to reposition the controls.

2. Click the **Toolbox button** on the Form Design toolbar to toggle it off (if necessary), click the **Field List button** to toggle it off (if necessary), place the pointer on the right edge of the form, then when the pointer changes to ↔, drag the right edge to the **6"** mark on the horizontal ruler

The form is expanded so that it is 6" wide, as shown in Figure C-5. Before moving, resizing, deleting, or changing a control in any way, you must select it.

3. Click the **PeoplesChoice check box**

Squares, called **sizing handles**, appear in the corners and on the edges of the selected control. When you work with controls, the mouse pointer shape is very important. Pointer shapes are summarized in Table C-2.

Trouble?

If you make a mistake, immediately click the Undo button and try again.

4. Place the pointer on the **selected control**, when the pointer changes to 👋, drag the control so that the left edge of the label is at the **4"** mark on the horizontal ruler and the bottom edge is aligned with the **RecordingID text box**

The text boxes appear as white rectangles in this form. When you move a bound control, such as a text box or check box, the accompanying unbound label control to its left moves with it. The field name for the selected control appears in the Object list box.

QuickTip

You can move controls one pixel at a time by pressing [Ctrl] and an arrow key. You can resize controls one pixel at a time by pressing [Shift] and an arrow key.

5. Select and move the **Quantity** and **Tracks text boxes** using the 👋 pointer to match their final locations as shown in Figure C-6

Resizing controls also improves the design of the form.

6. Click the **Retail text box**, then use the ↔ pointer to drag the middle-right edge sizing handle left to the **2"** mark, click the **Wholesale text box**, then drag the middle-right edge sizing handle left to the **2"** mark

Moving and resizing controls requires great concentration and mouse control. Don't worry if your screen doesn't *precisely* match the next figure, but *do* make sure that you understand how to use the move and resize mouse pointers used in Form Design view. Precision and accuracy are naturally developed with practice, but even experienced form designers regularly rely on the Undo button.

7. Click the **Form View button** on the Form Design toolbar, click the **Artist text box**, click the **Sort Descending button**, then click the **Sort Ascending button** on the Form View toolbar

Your screen should look like Figure C-7.

FIGURE C-5: **Design view of the Music Inventory form**

Form View button
Horizontal ruler
Field List button
Labels
Vertical ruler
Text boxes
Toolbox button
6" mark
Right edge of form

FIGURE C-6: **Controls have been moved**

Object list box
Text boxes have been moved
PeoplesChoice label and check box have been moved
"Move" mouse symbol

FIGURE C-7: **Reorganized Music Inventory form**

Check box
Text boxes
Labels

TABLE C-2: **Form Design view mouse pointer shapes**

shape	when does this shape appear?	action
	When you point to any nonselected control on the form; it is the default mouse pointer	Single-clicking with this mouse pointer *selects* a control
	When you point to the edge of a selected control (but not when you are pointing to a sizing handle)	Dragging this mouse pointer moves all selected controls
	When you point to the larger sizing handle in the upper-left corner of a selected control	Dragging this mouse pointer *moves only the single control* where pointer is currently positioned, not other controls that may also be selected
↔ ↕ ↖ ↗	When you point to any sizing handle (except the larger one in the upper-left corner)	Dragging this mouse pointer *resizes* the control

Modifying Labels

When you create a form with the Form Wizard, it places a label to the left of each text box with the field's name. Often, you'll want to modify those labels to be more descriptive or user friendly. You can modify a label control by directly editing it in Form Design view, or you can make the change in the label's property sheet. The **property sheet** is a comprehensive listing of all **properties** (characteristics) that have been specified for that control. ~~~~~ John modifies the Music Inventory form's labels to be more descriptive.

Steps

Trouble?

If you double-click a label, you will open its property sheet. Close the property sheet by clicking its Close button, then single-click the label again.

1. Click the **Design View button** 🖉 on the Form View toolbar, click the **RecordingID label** to select it, click between the **g** and **I** in the RecordingID label, then press **[Spacebar]** to insert a space

Directly editing labels in Form Design view is tricky because you must select the label and then precisely click where you want to edit it. You can also open the label's property sheet and modify the Caption property to change the displayed text.

2. Click the **Title label**, click the **Properties button** 🖭 on the Form Design toolbar, then click the **Format tab**, as shown in Figure C-8

The Caption property controls the text displayed by the label control, and the property can be found on either the Format or the All tabs. The All tab is an exhaustive list of all the properties for a control.

Trouble?

Be sure to modify the Title label control and not the Title text box control. Text box controls must reference the *exact* field name in order to display the data within that field.

3. Click to the left of **Title** in the Caption property text box, type **Recording**, press **[Spacebar]**, then click 🖭 to toggle the property sheet off

Don't be overwhelmed by the number of properties available for each control on the form. Over time, you may want to learn about most of these properties, but in the beginning, you'll be able to make the vast majority of the property changes through menu and toolbar options rather than by accessing the property sheet itself. Labels can be aligned so that they are closer to their respective text boxes.

4. Click the **Recording ID label**, then click the **Align Right button** 🗐 on the Formatting (Form/Report) toolbar

The Recording ID label is now much closer to its associated text box. See Table C-3 for a list of techniques to quickly select several controls so that you can apply alignment and formatting changes to many controls simultaneously.

5. Click the **0.5"** mark on the horizontal ruler to select the first column of controls, as shown in Figure C-9, then click 🗐

All the labels in the first column are right-aligned and next to their text boxes.

6. Click the **Save button** 🖬 on the Form Design toolbar, then click the **Form View button** 🖼 on the Form Design toolbar

The Music Inventory form is saved, and you can see that the labels are close to the data in the first column.

FIGURE C-8: Looking at a label's property sheet

Recording ID label has been changed

Title label is chosen

Caption property

Properties button

The property sheet title bar tells you what type of control you are working with

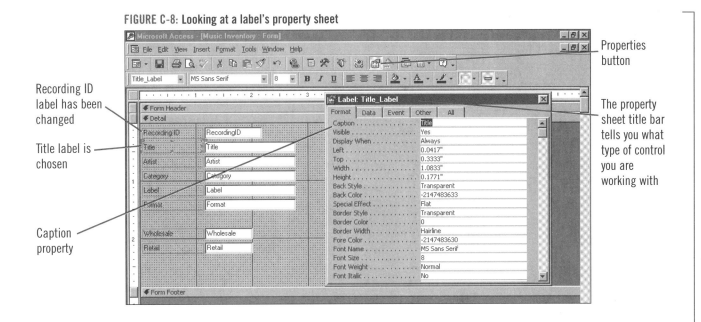

FIGURE C-9: Selecting several labels at the same time

Clicking the 0.5" mark on the ruler

All labels in the first column are selected

Formatting (Form/Report) toolbar

Align Right button

TABLE C-3: Selecting more than one control

technique	description
Click, [Shift]+click	Click a control, then press and hold [Shift] while clicking other controls; each one will be selected
Drag a selection box	If you drag a selection box (an imaginary box you create by dragging the pointer in Form Design view), every control that is in or touched by the edges of the box will be selected
Click in the ruler	If you click in either the horizontal or vertical ruler you will select all controls that intersect the selection line (an imaginary line you create by clicking the ruler)
Drag in the ruler	If you drag through either the horizontal or vertical ruler you will select all controls that intersect the selection line as it is dragged through the ruler

Modifying Text Boxes

Text boxes are generally used to display data from underlying fields and are therefore *bound* to that field. You can also use a text box as a calculated control which is not directly bound to a field but rather uses information from a field to calculate an answer. ✎ John wants the Music Inventory form to calculate the profit for each record. He uses a text box calculated control to find the difference between the Retail and Wholesale fields.

Steps 1 2 3 4

Trouble?

The Toolbox toolbar may be floating or docked on the edge of your screen. Drag the title bar of a floating toolbar or the top edge of a docked toolbar to move it to a convenient location.

Trouble?

The number in the caption "Text22" varies depending on how many controls you add to the form.

Trouble?

If your calculated control did not work, return to Design view, click the calculated control, press [Delete], then repeat steps 1 through 4.

Trouble?

Properties are not listed in alphabetical order so you may have to scroll up or down the property sheet to find the Format and Text Align properties.

1. Click the **Design View button** 📇 on the Form View toolbar, click the **Toolbox button** ⚒ on the Form View toolbar, click the **Text Box button** 🔲 on the Toolbox toolbar, the pointer changes to ⁺🔲, click just below the Retail text box on the form, then if necessary move the new text box and label control to align with the controls above it
   Your screen should look like Figure C-10. Adding a new text box *automatically* added a new label with the default caption "Text22:". You can access the text box's property sheet to bind it to an underlying field or expression, or you can create the calculated expression directly in the text box.

2. Click **Unbound** in the new text box, type **=[Retail]-[Wholesale]**, then press **[Enter]**
   When referencing field names within an expression, you *must* use square brackets and type the field name exactly as it appears in the Table Design view. You do not need to worry about uppercase and lowercase letters. The label for any expression should be descriptive.

3. Click the **Text22: label** to select it, click the **Text22: label** again to edit it, double-click **Text22**, type **Profit** as the new caption, then press **[Enter]**
   The calculated text box control and associated label are modified.

4. Click the **Form View button** 📇 to view your changes, click the **Ascending Sort button** 📇 on the Form View toolbar
   Your screen should look like Figure C-11. The first record is $5 wholesale and sells for $11.00 retail so the profit is calculated as $6. You can use Form Design view to make a few more changes to clarify the form.

5. Click 📇, click the **Calculated text box**, then click the **Properties button** 📇 on the Form Design toolbar
   By default, the values in text boxes that contain numeric and currency fields are right-aligned. Text boxes that contain fields with other data types or those that start as unbound controls are left-aligned. Monetary values should be right-aligned and display with a dollar sign and cents.

6. Click the **Format tab** in the Text Box property sheet, click the **Format property text box**, click the **Format property list arrow**, scroll and click **Currency**, click the **Text Align property text box**, scroll and click the **Text Align property list arrow**, then click **Right**

7. Click the **Properties button** 📇, switch the position of the **Retail and Wholesale text boxes**, move and align the **Profit label**, resize the **calculated text box** (as shown in Figure C-12), then click the **Form View button** 📇
   The calculated profit value should display as $6.00 and be right-aligned within the text box.

FIGURE C-10: **Adding a calculated text box**

Toolbox button

Toolbox toolbar

Click to add a
text box control

New label

New text box

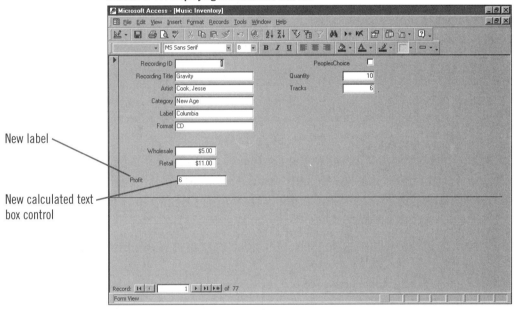

FIGURE C-11: **Displaying a calculated text box**

New label

New calculated text
box control

FIGURE C-12: **Updated Music Inventory form**

Retail and
Wholesale fields
are switched

Modifying Tab Order

Once all of the controls have been added, moved, and resized on the form, you'll want to check and probably modify the tab order. The **tab order** is the order in which the **focus** (the active control) moves as you press [Tab] in Form view. Since the form is the primary object by which users will view, edit, and enter data, careful attention to tab order is essential to maintain their productivity and satisfaction with the database. John checks the tab order of the Music Inventory form, then changes the tab order as necessary in Form Design view.

QuickTip

You can also press [Enter] to move the focus from field to field on a form.

1. **Press [Tab] 11 times watching the focus move through the bound controls of the form**
   Currently, focus moves back and forth between the left and right columns of controls. For efficient data entry, you want the focus to move down through the first column of text boxes before moving to the second column.

2. **Click the Design View button** ▨ **on the Form View toolbar, click View on the menu bar, then click Tab Order**
   The Tab Order dialog box opens in which you can drag fields up or down to change their tab sequence. The Tab Order dialog box allows you to change the tab order of controls in three sections: Form Header, Detail, and Form Footer. Right now, all of the controls are positioned in the form's Detail section. See Table C-4 for more information on form sections.

3. **Click the Retail row selector in the Custom Order list, drag it up to position it just below Format, click the Wholesale row selector, drag it under Retail, click the Tracks row selector, then drag it under Quantity as shown in Figure C-13**
   With the change made, test the new tab order.

4. **Click OK in the Tab Order dialog box, then click the Form View button** ▣ **on the Form Design toolbar**
   Although nothing visibly changes on the form, the tab order is different.

5. **Press [Enter] 10 times to move through the fields of the form with the new tab order**
   You should now be moving through all of the text boxes of the first column, with the exception of the calculated field, before you move to the second column.

6. **Click the Save button** ▣ **on the Form View toolbar**

FIGURE C-13: **Tab Order dialog box**

Tab Order
dialog box
with Detail
section
chosen

Form
Header
section

Detail
section

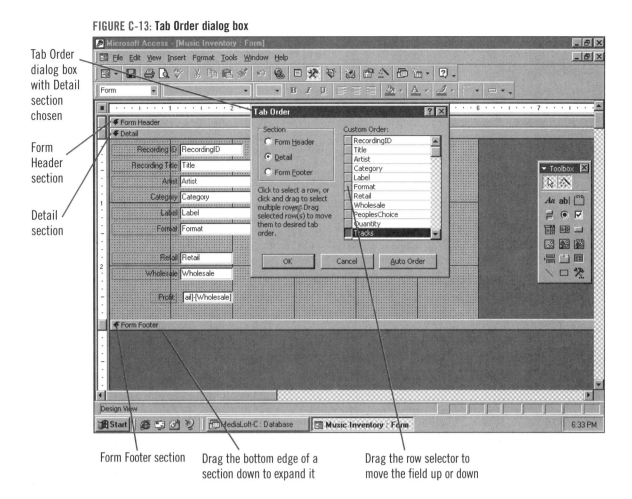

Form Footer section   Drag the bottom edge of a   Drag the row selector to
                         section down to expand it   move the field up or down

TABLE C-4: **Form sections**

section	description
Form Header	Controls placed in the Form Header print only once at the top of the printout; by default, this section is not "opened" in Form Design view, but can be expanded by dragging its bottom edge in Form Design view.
Detail	Controls placed in the Detail section print once for every record in the underlying table or query object; all controls created by the Form Wizard are placed in this section
Form Footer	Controls placed in the Form Footer print only once at the end of the printout; by default, this section is not "opened" in Form Design view, but it can be expanded by dragging its bottom edge down in Form Design view

Entering and Editing Records

The most important reasons for using a form are to find, enter, or edit records to the underlying object. You can also print a form, but you must be careful because printing a form often produces a very long printout because of the vertical orientation of the fields. ✎ John uses the Music Inventory form to add a new record to the underlying Music Inventory table. Then he prints the form with the data for only the new record.

Steps 1 2 3 4

QuickTip

A New Record button is also on the Navigation buttons.

1. Click the **New Record button** ⏭ on the Form View toolbar
A new, blank record is displayed. The text "(AutoNumber)" appears in the Recording ID field, which will automatically increment when you begin to enter data. The Specific Record box indicates the current record number.

QuickTip

To enter a check in a check box press [Spacebar].

2. Click the **Recording Title text box**, type **The Dance**, then enter the rest of the information shown in Figure C-14
Notice that the Profit text box shows the calculated result of $4.00. The new record is stored as record 78 in the Music Inventory table.

Trouble?

Don't click the Print button on the Form View toolbar because *all* of the records in the underlying object will print.

3. Click **File** on the menu bar, click **Print** to open the Print dialog box, click the **Selected Record(s) option button** in the Print Range section, then click **OK**
Forms are also often used to edit existing records in the database.

4. Click the **Recording Title text box**, click the **Find button** 🔍 on the Form View toolbar to open the Find and Replace dialog box, type **Mermaid Avenue** in the Find What text box, then click **Find Next**
Record 77 appears behind the Find and Replace dialog box, as shown in Figure C-15.

5. Click **Cancel** in the Find and Replace dialog box, press **[Tab]** five times to go to the Retail field, type **20**, then press **[Tab]**
Editing either the Wholesale or Retail fields automatically updates the calculated Profit field. Forms are also a great way to filter the records to a specific subset.

6. Click **Pop** in the Category text box, then click the **Filter By Selection button** 🍋 on the Form View toolbar
Twelve records were found that matched the "Pop" criteria. Previewing the records helps to determine how many pages the printout would be.

7. Click the **Print Preview button** 🔍 on the Form View toolbar
Since about three records print on a page, your printout would be four pages long.

8. Click the **Close button** on the Print Preview toolbar, then click the **Remove Filter button** 🔽 on the Form View toolbar so that all 78 records in the Music Inventory table are available

FIGURE C-14: Entering a new record into a form

Edit record symbol

New Record button

Calculated text box automatically displays the answer

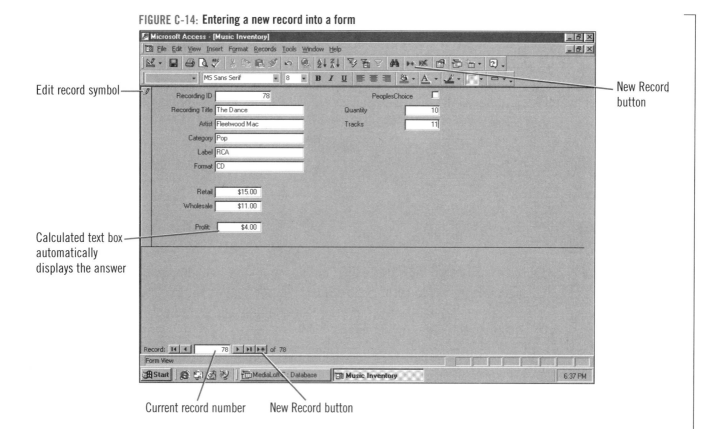

Current record number   New Record button

FIGURE C-15: Finding "Mermaid Avenue" using a form

Mermaid Avenue found in Title field

Find button

Record 77

Inserting an Image

Graphic images, such as pictures, a logo, or clip art, can add style and professionalism to a form. If you add a graphic image as an unbound image to the Form Header, the image will appear at the top of the form in Form view and once at the top of the printout when printing records through a form. ◥━━━ John adds the MediaLoft logo and a descriptive title to the Form Header section.

Steps 1234

1. Click the **Design View button** 🖼 on the Form View toolbar, place the pointer on the bottom edge of the Form Header, the pointer changes to ✛, then drag the bottom of the Form Header section to the 1" mark on the vertical ruler
   The Form Header section is open.

2. Click the **Image button** 🖼 on the Toolbox toolbar, the pointer changes to ⁺🖼, then click in the **Form Header section** at the 1" mark on the horizontal ruler
   The Insert Picture dialog box opens. The MediaLoft image file you want to insert in the Form Header is on the Project Disk.

3. Click the **Look in list arrow**, click the drive containing your Project Disk, click **smallmedia**, then click **OK**
   The MediaLoft logo appears in the Form Header, surrounded by handles, as shown in Figure C-16. Form header titles add a finishing touch to a form.

4. Click the **Label button** 🄰 on the Toolbox toolbar, the pointer changes to ⁺A, click to the right of the **MediaLoft logo** in the Form Header section, type **MediaLoft Music**, then press **[Enter]**
   Labels can be formatted to enhance the appearance on the form.

5. Click the **Font Size list arrow**, click **24**, point to the **upper-right resizing handle**, then drag the ↗ pointer so that the label **MediaLoft Music** is completely displayed
   If you double-click a label's sizing handle, the label will automatically adjust to display the entire caption.

6. Click the **Form View button** 🖼 on the Form Design toolbar
   You can go directly to a specific record by typing the record number in the specific record box.

7. Click in the **specific record box** on the Record Navigation buttons, type **11**, then press **[Enter]**
   Compare your form with Figure C-17.

8. Click **File** on the menu bar, click **Print**, click the **Selected Record(s) option button**, then click **OK**

9. Click the **Close button** on the Music Inventory form, then click **Yes** to save any changes if necessary

10. Close the MediaLoft-C database, then exit Access

FIGURE C-16: Adding an image to the Form Header section

1" mark on the ruler

MediaLoft logo

Label button

Image button

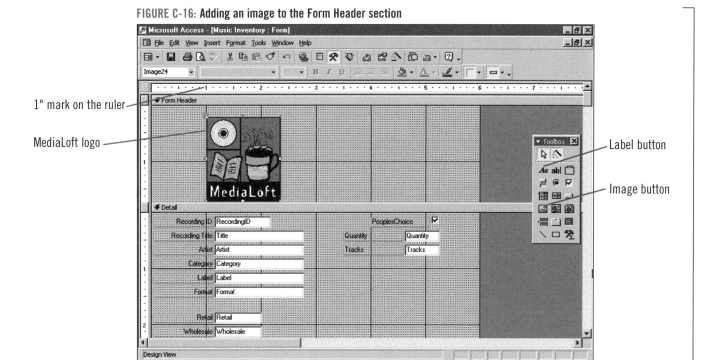

FIGURE C-17: The final Music Inventory form

MediaLoft logo

New label serves as form title

Form Header section

Creating a hyperlink from an image

Once an image is added to a form, you can convert it to a hyperlink by using its property sheet to modify the control's **Hyperlink Address** property in Form Design view. Depending on what you enter for the Hyperlink Address property, clicking the hyperlinked image in Form view opens another file, Access object, Web address, or e-mail address. For example, C:\Colleges\JCCCDescriptions.doc is the Hyperlink Address property entry to link a Word document at the specified drive and folder location; http://www.jccc.net creates a link between the image and the specified Web address.

Practice

► Concepts Review

Label each element of the Form Design window shown in Figure C-18.

FIGURE C-18

Match each term with the statement that describes it.

8. Sizing handles

9. Detail section

10. Bound control

11. Tab order

12. Form

13. Calculated control

a. An Access database object that allows you to arrange the fields of a record in any layout; you use it to enter, edit, and delete records

b. Displays data from a field in the underlying record source

c. Black squares that appear in the corners and edges of the selected control

d. The way in which the focus moves from one bound control to the next

e. Uses a text box and an expression to display an answer

f. Controls placed here print once for every record in the underlying table or query object

Select the best answer from the list of choices.

14. Every element on a form is called a
  a. Property.
  b. Control.
  c. Piece.
  d. Handle.

15. The pointer used to resize a control is
  a. ✛
  b. ↔
  c. ✋
  d. ☝

16. The most common bound control is the
  a. Label.
  b. Text box.
  c. Combo box.
  d. Check box.

17. The most common unbound control is the
  a. Label.
  b. Text box.
  c. Combo box.
  d. Image.

18. The _____ view is used to modify form controls.
  a. Form
  b. Datasheet
  c. Print Preview
  d. Design

► Skills Review

1. Plan a form.
   a. Plan a form to use for the data entry of business contacts by looking at several business cards.
   b. Write down the organization of the fields on the form. Determine what type of control you will use for each bound field.
   c. Identify the labels you would like to display on the form.

2. Create a form.
   a. Start Access and open the Membership-C database from your Project Disk.
   b. Click the Forms button in the Membership-C Database window, then double-click the Create form by using wizard option.
   c. Base the form on the Contacts table, and include all of the fields.
   d. Use a Columnar layout, a Standard style, and title the form "Contact Entry Form."
   e. Display the form with data.

3. Move and resize controls.
   a. Open and maximize the Design View window for the Contact Entry Form.
   b. Widen the form so that the right edge is at the 6" mark on the horizontal ruler.
   c. Move the LNAME text box and corresponding label to the right of the FNAME text box.
   d. Move the DUESOWED and DUESPAID text boxes and corresponding labels to the right of the address controls.
   e. Resize the PHONE and ZIP text boxes to be the same size as the CITY text box.
   f. Move the PHONE text box and corresponding label between the FNAME and COMPANY controls.

4. Modify labels.
   a. Right align all of the labels.
   b. Modify the FNAME label to FIRST NAME, the LNAME label to LAST NAME, the DUESOWED label to DUES OWED, and the DUESPAID label to DUES PAID.

5. Modify text boxes.
   a. Add a new text box below the DUESPAID text box.
   b. Type the expression =[DUESOWED]-[DUESPAID] in the new unbound text box. (*Hint*: Remember that you must use the *exact field names* in a calculated expression.)
   c. In the property sheet for the new calculated control, change the Format property to Currency.
   d. Right align the new calculated text boxes.
   e. Change the calculated text box label from Text20: to BALANCE.
   f. Move and resize the new calculated control and label so that it is aligned beneath the DUESOWED and DUES-PAID controls.

6. Modify tab order.
   a. Change the Tab order so that pressing [Tab] moves the focus through the text boxes in the following order: FNAME, LNAME, PHONE, COMPANY, STREET, CITY, STATE, ZIP, DUESOWED, DUESPAID, BALANCE text box

7. Enter and edit records.

a. Use the Contact Entry Form to enter the following new records:

	FIRST NAME	LAST NAME	PHONE	COMPANY	STREET
Record 1	Jane	Eagan	555-1166	Cummins Construction	1515 Maple St.
Record 2	Mark	Daniels	555-2277	Motorola	1010 Green St.

	CITY	STATE	ZIP	DUES OWED	DUES PAID
1 con't.	Fontanelle	KS	50033-	$50.00	$25.00
2 con't.	Bridgewater	KS	50022-	$50.00	$50.00

b. Print the Mark Daniels record.

c. Find the Lois Goode record, enter IBM in the Company text box, then print that record.

d. Filter for all records with a Zip entry of 64145. How many records did you find?

e. Sort the filtered 64145 zip code records in ascending order by Last Name, then print the first one.

8. Insert an image.

a. In Form Design view, expand the Form Header section to the 1" mark on the vertical ruler.

b. Use the Image control to insert the handin1.bmp file found on your Project Disk in the Form Header.

c. Centered and below the graphic file, add the label MEMBERSHIP INFORMATION in a 24-point font. Be sure to resize the label so that all of the text is visible.

d. Add your name as a label in the Form Header section.

e. View the form using the Form view.

f. Print the selected record.

g. Close the form, close the database, then exit Access.

► Independent Challenges

1. As the office manager of a cardiology clinic, you need to create a new patient data entry form. To complete this independent challenge:

a. Open the Clinic-C database from your Project Disk.

b. Using the Form Wizard, create a form that includes all the fields in the Demographics table, using the Columnar layout and Standard style. Title the form "Patient Entry Form."

c. In Form Design view, widen the form to the 6" mark, then move the DOB, Gender, Ins Code, and Entry Date controls to a second column to the right of the existing column. DOB should be next to Last Name.

d. Switch the positions of the State and Zip controls.

e. Modify the Medical Record Number label to MR Number, the Address 1 label to Address, the DOB label to Birthday, and the Ins Code label to Insurance.

f. Change the tab order so State is above Zip.

g. Use the newly created form to add a record using your own personal information. Enter 2000 for the MR Number, BCBS for the Insurance, and 2/1/00 for the Entry Date.

h. Print the form with the new record you just added about yourself.

i. Close the Patient Entry Form, close the Clinic-C database, then exit Access.

2. As office manager of a cardiology clinic you want to build a form that quickly calculates a height to weight ratio value based on information in the Outcomes Data table.

To complete this independent challenge:

a. Open the Clinic-C database from your Project Disk.

b. Using the Form Wizard, create a form based on the Outcomes Data table with only the following fields: MR#, Height, and Weight.

c. Use the Columnar layout and Standard style, and name the form "Height to Weight Ratio Form."

d. In Design view, widen the form to the 4" mark on the horizontal ruler, then add a text box to the right half of the form.

e. Close the Field list if necessary.

f. Enter the expression =[Height]/[Weight] in the unbound text box.

g. Modify the calculated expression's label from Text6: (the number may vary) to Ratio.

h. Resize the Ratio label so that it is closer to the calculated expression control, then right-align the Ratio label.

i. Change the format property of the calculated control to Fixed.

j. Open the form header and enter your name as a label.

k. View the form.

l. Print the form for the record for MR# 006494.

m. Sort the records in descending order by Height, then print the record with the tallest height entry.

n. Close the Height to Weight Ratio Form, close the Clinic-C database, then exit Access.

3. As office manager of a cardiology clinic you want to build a form to enter new insurance information.

To complete this independent challenge:

a. Open the Clinic-C database from your Project Disk.

b. Using the Form Wizard, create a form based on the Insurance Company Information table, and include all of the fields.

c. Use the Columnar layout, Standard style, and accept the default title for the form "Insurance Company Information."

d. Change the label Insurance Company Name to just "Insurance Company."

e. Resize the State text box so that it is the same size as the City text box.

f. Expand the Form Header section, and add the graphic image Medical.bmp found on your Project Disk to the left side of the Form Header section.

g. Add a label "Insurance Entry Form" and another for your name to the right of the medical clip art in the Form Header section.

h. Increase the size of the Insurance Entry Form label to 18 points. Resize the label to display the entire caption.

i. Switch to Form view, then find and print the Cigna record.

j. Filter for all records with a State entry of KS. Print those records.

k. Close the Insurance Company Information Form, close the Clinic-C database, then exit Access.

4. As a new employee in the Market Research department for MediaLoft, you use the World Wide Web to find information on competitors' Web sites, specifically as it relates to Web-based forms.

To complete this independent challenge:

a. Connect to the Internet, use your browser to go to the MediaLoft intranet site at http://www.course.com/illustrated/ MediaLoft, then click the link for the Research Center.

b. Click the link for www.amazon.com, and explore its Web site until you find a Web-based form that requests information about you as a customer or an order that you'd like to place. Print that online form.

c. Use the MediaLoft Research Center to find the home pages of at least three other Internet-based book and/or music stores.

d. Find and print one Web-based data entry form from each of the three sites that you found. (*Note*: You may have to pretend that you are actually making an online purchase in order to view and print these forms, so be sure to cancel the transaction if you do not intend to purchase any products. Never enter credit card or payment information if you are not serious about finalizing the sale.)

e. Disconnect from the Internet.

f. Draw a sketch to design a form that MediaLoft can use to take orders online. You can use the Music Inventory table in the MediaLoft database as your guide for product information.

g. List all the fields, the data types, and any labels and images for your order form.

Access 2000 | **Practice**

▶ Visual Workshop

Using the Clinic-C database, create the form based on the Demographics table, as shown in Figure C-19. Notice that the label "Patient Form" is 24 points and has been placed in the Form Header section. The clip art, medstaff.bmp, can be found on the Project Disk. The image has been placed on the right side of the Detail section, and many controls had to be resized in order for it to fit. Also notice that the labels are right-aligned. You also need to correct the gender entry for this record.

FIGURE C-19

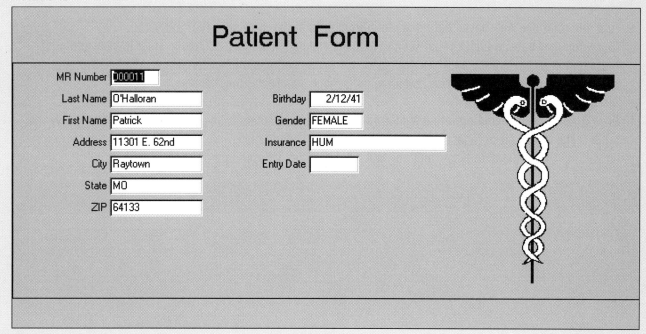

ACCESS C-24 **USING FORMS**

Using

Reports

Objectives

- MOUS ► **Plan a report**
- MOUS ► **Create a report**
- MOUS ► **Group records**
- MOUS ► **Change the sort order**
- MOUS ► **Modify an expression**
- MOUS ► **Align controls**
- MOUS ► **Format controls**
- ► **Create mailing labels**

A **report** is an Access object used to create printouts. You cannot enter or edit data through a report. Although data displayed in a report can be viewed on the screen, it is usually sent to a printer. Access reports can be based on the fields and records of either a table or a query object, can include extensive formatting embellishments such as clip art and lines, and can include professional headers and footers. Reports can also include meaningful calculations such as subtotals on groups of records. John Kim wants to produce reports that he can distribute to MediaLoft employees who do not yet have access to the MediaLoft database.

Planning a Report

Without clear communication, the accuracy and integrity of information being discussed can be questioned, misinterpreted, or obscured. Hard copy reports are often the primary tool used to communicate database information at meetings, with outsiders, and with top executives. Although the **Report Wizard** can help you create an initial report object that you can later modify, the time spent planning your report not only increases your productivity but also ensures that the overall report meets its intended objectives. ✐ John has been asked to provide several reports on a regular basis to the MediaLoft executives. He plans his first report that summarizes inventory quantities within each music category.

John uses the following guidelines to plan his report:

Identify a meaningful title for the report

The title should clearly identify the purpose of the report and be meaningful to those who will be reading the report. The title is created with a label control placed in the **Report Header** section. **Sections** are the parts of the report that determine where a control will display on the report. See Table D-1 for more information on report sections. Just like forms, every element on a report is a control.

Determine the information (the fields and records) that the report will show

You can base a report on a table, but usually you create a query to gather the specific fields from the one or more tables upon which to base the report. Of course, using a query also allows you to set criteria to limit the number of records displayed by the report.

Determine how the fields should be laid out on the report

Most reports display fields in a horizontal layout across the page, but you can arrange them in any way you want. Just as in forms, bound text box controls are used on a report to display the data stored in the underlying records. These text boxes are generally placed in the report **Detail** section.

Determine how the records should be sorted and/or grouped within the report

In an Access report, the term **grouping** refers to sorting records *plus* providing a section before the group of records called the **Group Header** section and a section after the group of records called the **Group Footer** section. These sections include additional controls that often contain calculated expressions such as a subtotal for a group of records. The ability to group records is extremely powerful and only available through the report object.

Identify any other descriptive information that should be placed at the end of the report or at the top or bottom of each page

You will use the **Report Footer**, **Page Header**, and **Page Footer** sections for these descriptive controls. John has sketched his first report in Figure D-1.

FIGURE D-1: Sketch of the Quantities Report

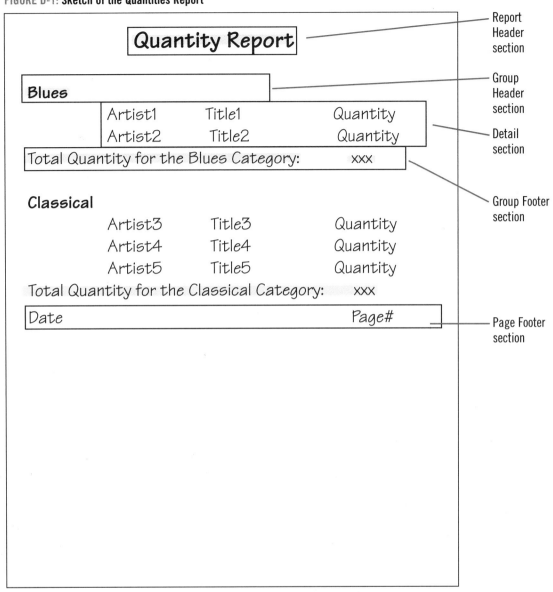

TABLE D-1: Report sections

section	where does this section print?	which controls are most commonly placed there?
Report Header	At the top of the first page of the report	Label controls containing the report title; can also include clip art, a logo image, or a line separating the title from the rest of the report
Page Header	At the top of every page (but below the report header on page one)	Descriptive label controls often acting as column headings for text box controls in the Detail section
Group Header	Before every group of records	Text box control for the field by which the records are grouped
Detail	Once for every record	Text box controls for the rest of the fields
Group Footer	After every group of records	Text box controls containing calculated expressions, such as subtotals or counts, for the records in that group
Page Footer	At the bottom of every page	Text box controls containing page number or date expression
Report Footer	At the end of the entire report	Text box controls containing expressions such as grand totals or counts that calculate an answer for all of the records in the report

Creating a Report

You can create reports in Access in **Report Design view**, or you can use the **Report Wizard** to help you get started. The Report Wizard asks questions that guide you through the initial development of the report, similar to the Form Wizard. In addition to questions about which object the report is based, which fields you want to view in the report, and the style and layout of the report, the Report Wizard also asks how you want report records to be grouped and sorted. ➤ John uses the Report Wizard to create the Quantities Report he planned on paper.

1. Start Access, click the **Open an existing file option button**, then open the **MediaLoft-D** database from your Project Disk
   This database contains an enhanced Music Inventory table and several queries from which you will base your reports.

2. Click **Reports** on the Objects bar in the MediaLoft-D Database window, then double-click **Create report by using wizard**
   The Report Wizard dialog box opens. You'll use the Selection Quantities query for this report. Another way to quickly create a report is by selecting a table or query, clicking the New Object list arrow on the Database toolbar and then selecting AutoReport. AutoReport, however, does not give you a chance to review the options provided by the Report Wizard.

3. Click the **Tables/Queries list arrow**, click **Query: Selection Quantities**, click **Category** in the Available Fields list, click the **Select Single Field button** ▶, click **Title**, click ▶, click **Artist**, click ▶, click **Quantity**, then click ▶
   The first dialog box of the Report Wizard should look like Figure D-2. The Report Wizard also asks grouping and sorting questions that determine the order and amount of detail provided on the report.

   Trouble?
   You can always click Back to review previous dialog boxes within a wizard.

4. Click **Next**, click **Next** to move past the grouping levels question, click the **first sort order list arrow** in the sort order dialog box, then click **Category**
   At this point you have not specified any grouping fields, but specified that you want the fields sorted by Category. You can use the Report Wizard to specify up to four sort fields in either an ascending or descending sort order for each field.

5. Click **Next**, click **Next** to accept the **Tabular** layout and **Portrait** orientation, click **Corporate** for the style, click **Next**, type **Quantities Report** for the report title, verify that the **Preview the report option button** is selected, then click **Finish**
   The Quantities Report opens in Print Preview, as shown in Figure D-3. It is very similar to the sketch created earlier. Notice that the records are sorted by the Category field.

Why reports should be based on queries

Although you can use the first dialog box of the Report Wizard to select fields from different tables without first creating a query to collect those fields into one object, it is not recommended. If you later decide that you want to add more fields to the report or limit the number of records in the table, you will find it very easy to add fields or criteria to an underlying query object to meet these new needs. To accomplish this same task without using an intermediary query object requires that you change the properties of the report itself, which most users find more difficult.

FIGURE D-2: **First Report Wizard dialog box**

Base the report on
the Selection
Quantities query

Select Single Field
button

Fields selected for
the report

FIGURE D-3: **Quantities Report in Print Preview**

Report Header

Page Header

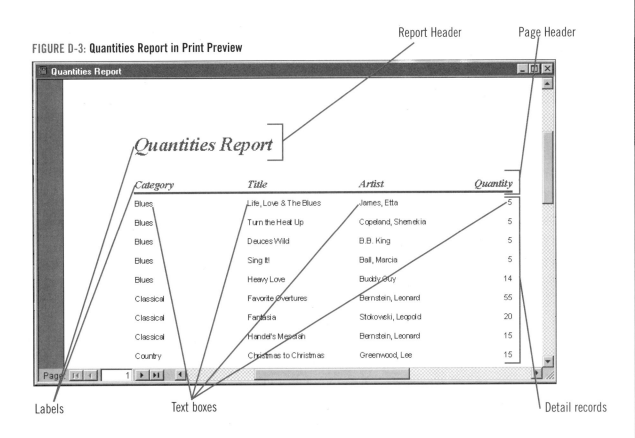

Labels

Text boxes

Detail records

Grouping Records

Grouping refers to sorting records on a report *plus* providing an area above and below the group of records in which additional controls can be placed. These two sections of the report are called the Group Header and Group Footer. You can create groups on a report through the Report Wizard, or you can change an existing report's grouping and sorting fields in Report Design view. Just as with forms, you make all structural changes to a report in the object's Design view. John wants to group the Quantities Report by Category instead of simply sorting it by Category. In addition, he wants to add controls to the Group Header and Group Footer to clarify and summarize information within the report.

Trouble?

If a property has a predetermined set of options, a list arrow will display when you click that property's text box in the property sheet.

1. **Click the Design View button** ⬚ **on the Print Preview toolbar to switch to Report Design view, as shown in Figure D-4**
   Report Design view shows you the sections of the report as well as the controls within each section. Labels and text boxes are formatted similarly in Report Design view. You can click a control and then click the Properties button to view the title bar of the property sheet to determine the nature of a control. Report Design view is where you change grouping and sort fields.

2. **Click the Sorting and Grouping button** ⬚ **on the Report Design toolbar, click the Group Header text box, click the Group Header list arrow, click Yes, click the Group Footer text box, click the Group Footer list arrow, then click Yes**
   Specifying "Yes" for the Group Header and Group Footer properties opens those sections of the report in Report Design view.

3. **Click** ⬚ **to close the dialog box, click the Category text box in the Detail section, then drag the textbox with the** 🖑 **pointer directly up into the Category Header section**
   By placing the Category text box in the Category Header, it will print once for each new group rather than once for each record. You can add calculated subtotal controls for each category of records by placing a text box in the Category Footer section.

QuickTip

The Field list, Toolbox toolbar, and property sheet may or may not be visible, but you can turn them on and off by clicking their respective toggle buttons. You can move them by dragging their title bars.

4. **If the Toolbox toolbar is not visible, click the Toolbox button** ⬚ **on the Report Design toolbar, click the Text Box button** ⬚ **on the Toolbox toolbar, then click in the Category Footer section directly below the Quantity text box**
   Your screen should look like Figure D-5. You can use the label and text box controls in the Category Footer section to describe and subtotal the Quantity field respectively.

5. **Click the Text13: label in the Category Footer section to select it, double-click Text13, type Subtotal, then press [Enter]**

Trouble?

If you double-click the edge of a control, you open the control's property sheet.

6. **Click the unbound text box control in the Category Footer section to select it, click the unbound text box control again to edit it, then type =sum([Quantity])**
   The expression that calculates the sum of the Quantity field is now in the unbound text box control. Calculated expressions start with an equal sign. When entering an expression, the field name must be referenced exactly and surrounded by square brackets.

7. **Click the Print Preview button** ⬚ **on the Report Design toolbar, then scroll through the report as necessary**
   The new report that groups and summarizes records by Category appears, as shown in Figure D-6. Since the Category text box was moved to the Category Header section, it prints only once per group of records. Each group of records is trailed by a Group Footer that includes the Subtotal label as well as a calculated field that subtotals the Quantity field.

8. **Click Close on the Print Preview toolbar, click the Save button** ⬚ **, then click the Quantities Report Close button to close the report**
   The Quantities Report is now an object in the MediaLoft-D Database window.

FIGURE D-4: **Quantities Report Design view**

Field List button

Toolbox button

Sorting and Grouping button

Properties button

Sections

Labels

Toolbox toolbar

Text boxes

Field list

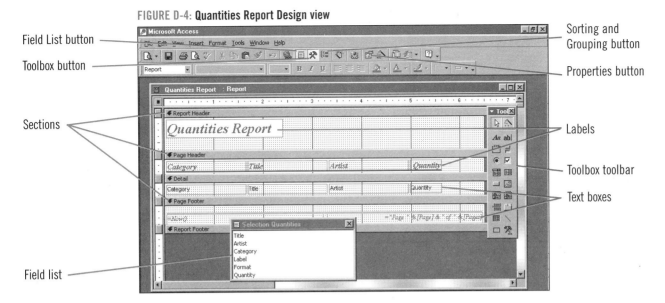

FIGURE D-5: **Adding controls to the group footer section**

Text Box button

Category Header

Category text box moved up from Detail section into Category Header section

New text box

Category Footer

New label

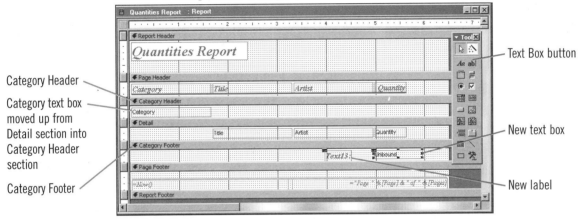

FIGURE D-6: **The Quantities Report grouped by Category**

Group Header (Category is the grouping field)

Report Header

Page Header

Detail

Group Footer (Category is the grouping field)

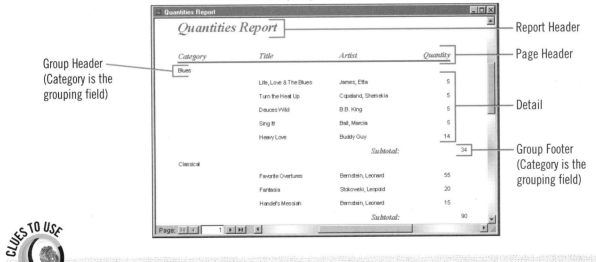

CLUES TO USE

Adding a field to a report

Clicking the Field List button 🔲 on the Report Design toolbar toggles the field list of the underlying table or query object. To add a field from this list to the report, simply drag it from the Field list to the appropriate position on the report. This action creates both a label control that displays the field name and a text box control that displays the value of the field from the underlying records.

Changing the Sort Order

Grouping records is really just sorting them with the additional ability to create a Group Header or Group Footer section on the report. The grouping field acts as a primary sort field. You can define further sort fields too. When you further sort records within a group, you order the Detail records according to a particular field. The Report Wizard prompts you for group and sort information at the time you create the report, but you can also group and sort an existing report by using the Sorting and Grouping dialog box in Report Design view. John wants to modify the Quantities Report so that the Detail records are sorted by the Artist field within the Category group.

Steps

1. Click the **Quantities Report** in the MediaLoft-D Database window, then click the **Design button**
   The Quantities Report opens in Report Design view.

2. Click the **Sorting and Grouping button** on the Report Design toolbar, click the **second row Field/Expression text box**, click the **Field/Expression list arrow**, then click **Artist**
   The Sorting and Grouping dialog box looks like Figure D-7. There is no Sorting and Grouping indicator in the Artist row selector. Both the Group Header and Group Footer Group properties are "No" which indicates that the Artist field is providing a sort order only.

3. Click to toggle the Sorting and Grouping dialog box off, then click the **Print Preview button** on the Report Design toolbar
   Part of the report is shown in Print Preview, as shown in Figure D-8. You can use the buttons on the Print Preview toolbar to view more of the report.

4. Click the **One Page button** on the Print Preview toolbar to view one miniature page, click the **Two Pages button** to view two miniature pages, click the **Multiple Pages button**, then drag to **1x4 Pages** in the grid as shown in Figure D-9
   The Print Preview window displays the four pages of the report in miniature. Regardless of the zoom magnification of the pages, however, you can click the **Zoom pointer** to quickly toggle between two zoom magnifications.

5. Point to the **last subtotal** on the last page of the report with the pointer, click to read the number **92**, then click again to return the report to its former four-page magnification level

6. Click the **Close** button on the Print Preview toolbar, then click the **Save button** on the Report Design toolbar

FIGURE D-7: Specifying a sort order

Sorting and Grouping indicator

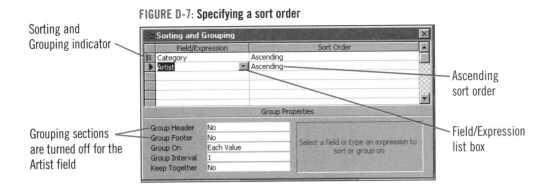

Ascending sort order

Grouping sections are turned off for the Artist field

Field/Expression list box

FIGURE D-8: The Quantities Report sorted by Artist

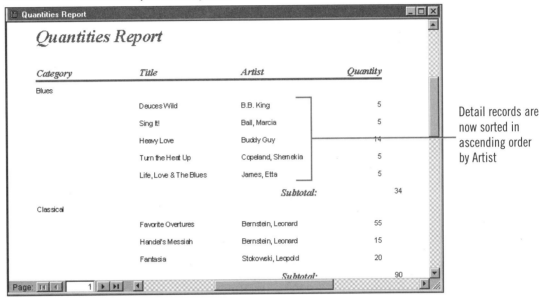

Detail records are now sorted in ascending order by Artist

FIGURE D-9: Print Preview

One Page button

Two Pages button

Multiple Pages button

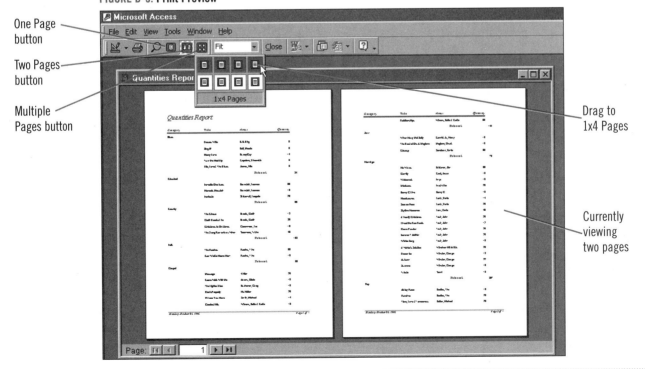

Drag to 1x4 Pages

Currently viewing two pages

Modifying an Expression

An **expression** is a combination of fields, operators (such as +, -, / and *) and functions that result in a single value. A **function** is a built-in formula provided by Access that helps you quickly create a calculated expression. See Table D-2 for examples of common expressions that use Access functions. Notice that every calculated expression starts with an equal sign, and when it uses a function, the arguments for the function are placed in parentheses. **Arguments** are the pieces of information that the function needs to create the final answer. Calculated expressions are entered in text box controls. ✐ John adds a calculated expression to the Quantities Report that uses the Count function to count the number of records within each music category.

Steps

1. Make sure the Quantities Report is in Report Design view, click the **=Sum([Quantity])** **text box** in the Category Footer section, click the **Copy button** 📇 on the Report Design toolbar, click in a **blank area** in the left part of the Category Footer section, then click the **Paste button** 📋 on the Report Design toolbar
   The text box and accompanying label are copied and pasted, as shown in Figure D-10. Modifying a copy of the existing calculated expression control helps reduce errors and saves on keystrokes.

2. Click the copied **Subtotal label** in the Category Footer section to select it, double-click **Subtotal** to select the text, type **Count**, then press **[Enter]**
   The label is only descriptive text. The text box is the control that actually calculates the count.

3. Click the copy of the **=Sum([Quantity])** **text box** to select it, double-click **Sum** to select it, type **count**, then press **[Enter]**
   The expression now counts the number of records in each group.

4. Click the **Print Preview button** 🔍 on the Report Design toolbar to view the updated report, click the **One Page button** 🔲 on the Print Preview toolbar, then scroll and zoom as shown in Figure D-11

Using the Office Clipboard

The Office Clipboard works together with the Windows Clipboard to let you copy and paste multiple items within or between the Office applications. The Office Clipboard can hold up to 12 items copied or cut from any Office program. The Clipboard toolbar displays the items stored on the Office Clipboard. The collected items remain on the Clipboard and are available to you until you close all open Office applications.

FIGURE D-10: Copying and pasting a calculated control

Copy button

Paste button

New label control

New text box control

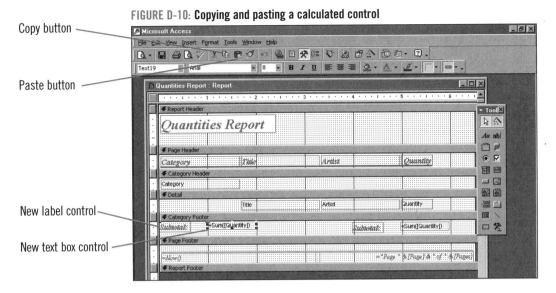

FIGURE D-11: Previewing the Count calculated control

New label control

New text box control

TABLE D-2: Common Access expressions

category	sample expression	description
Arithmetic	=[Price]*1.05	Multiplies the Price field by 1.05 (adds 5% to the Price field)
Arithmetic	=[Subtotal]+[Shipping]	Adds the value of the Subtotal field to the value of the Shipping field
Page Number	=[Page]	Displays the current page number, such as 5, 6, or 10
Page Number	="Page "&[Page]	Displays the word "Page," a space, and the current page number, such as Page 5, Page 6, or Page 10
Text	=[FirstName]&" "&[LastName]	Displays the value of the FirstName and LastName fields in one control separated by a space
Text	=Left([ProductNumber],2)	Uses the **Left** function to display the first two characters in the ProductNumber field
Aggregate	=Avg([Freight])	Uses the **Avg** function to display an average of the values in the Freight field
Aggregate	=Count([FirstName])	Uses the **Count** function to display the number of records that contain an entry in the FirstName field
Aggregate	=Sum([Tracks])	Uses the **Sum** function to display the total value from the Tracks field
Date	=Date()	Uses the **Date** function to display the current date in the form of mm-dd-yy, such as 10-23-00 or 11-14-01

Aligning Controls

Once the information that you want to present has been added to the appropriate section of a report, you may also want to rearrange the data on the report. By aligning controls in columns and rows, you can present your information so it is easier to understand. There are several **alignment** commands that are important to understand. You can left-, right-, or center-align a control *within its own border*, or you can align the edges of controls *with respect to one another*. ◢◤ John aligns several controls on the Quantities Report to improve the readability and professionalism of the report. His first task is to right-align all of the controls in the Category Footer.

Steps 123 4

1. Click the **Design View button** 🖳 on the Print Preview toolbar, then click in the vertical ruler to the left of the Count label in the Category Footer section
   All four controls in the Category Footer section are selected. Text boxes that display numeric fields are right-aligned by default; the labels and text boxes you added in the Category Footer section that display calculated expressions are left-aligned by default. You can use the same techniques for selecting controls in Report Design view as you did in Form Design view.

2. Click the **Align Right button** ▤ on the Formatting (Form/Report) toolbar
   Your screen should look like Figure D-12. Now the information displayed by the control is right-aligned within the control.

3. With the four controls still selected, click **Format** on the menu bar, point to **Align**, then click **Bottom**
   The bottom edges of the four controls are now aligned with respect to one another. The Align command on the Format menu refers to aligning controls with respect to one another. The Alignment buttons on the Formatting toolbar refer to aligning controls within their own borders. You can also align the right or left edges of controls in different sections.

4. Click the **Quantity label** in the Page Header section, press and hold [Shift], click the **Quantity text box** in the Detail section, click the **=Sum([Quantity])** text box in the Category Footer section, release [Shift], click **Format** on the menu bar, point to **Align**, then click **Right**
   The right edges of the Quantity label, Quantity text box, and Quantity calculated controls are aligned. With the edges at the same position and the information right-aligned within the controls, the controls form a perfect column on the final report. You can extend the line in the Page Header section to better define the sections on the page.

Trouble?

Don't drag beyond the 6"
mark or the printout will be
wider than one sheet of paper.

5. Click the **blue line** in the Page Header section, press and hold [Shift], point to the **right sizing handle**, when the pointer changes to ↖, drag the handle to the **6" mark**, then release [Shift]
   By pressing [Shift] when you draw or resize a line, the line remains perfectly horizontal as you drag it left or right.

6. Click the **Print Preview button** 🔍 on the Report Design toolbar, then scroll and zoom
   Your screen should look like Figure D-13.

FIGURE D-12: **Working with the alignment buttons**

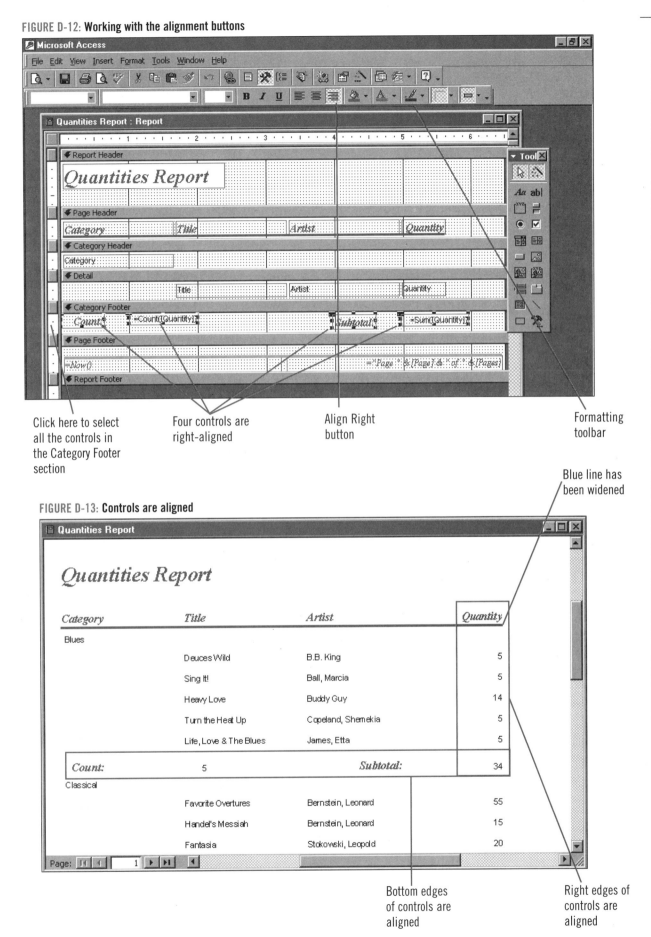

Click here to select all the controls in the Category Footer section

Four controls are right-aligned

Align Right button

Formatting toolbar

Blue line has been widened

FIGURE D-13: **Controls are aligned**

Bottom edges of controls are aligned

Right edges of controls are aligned

Formatting Controls

Formatting refers to enhancing the appearance of the information. Table D-3 lists several of the most popular formatting commands which can be used with either forms or reports. Although the Report Wizard provides many formatting embellishments on a report, you often want to improve upon the report's appearance to fit your particular needs. ➡ John doesn't feel that the music category information is prominent on the report, so he wants to format that control to change its appearance.

1. Click the **Design View button** on the Print Preview toolbar, click the **Toolbox button** to toggle it off, then click the **Category text box** in the Category Header section
   Before you can format any control, it must be selected.

2. Click the **Font size list arrow** on the Formatting (Form/Report) toolbar, click **11**, then click the **Bold button** B
   Increasing the font size and applying bold are common ways to make information more visible on a report. You can also change the colors of the control.

3. With the Category text box still selected, click the **Font/Fore Color list arrow** A·, then click the **Red box** (third row, first column on the left), as shown in Figure D-14
   Many buttons on the Formatting (Form/Report) toolbar include a list arrow that you can click to reveal a list of choices. When you click the color list arrow, a palette of available colors is displayed. You can change the background color of the Category text box using the palette.

4. With the Category text box still selected, click the **Fill/Back Color list arrow** ·, then click the **light gray box** (fourth row, first column on the right)
   When you print colors on a black and white printer, they become various shades of gray. So unless you always print to a color printer, be careful about relying too heavily on color formatting, especially background shades that often become solid black boxes when printed on a black and white printer or fax machine. Fortunately, Access allows you to undo your last command if you don't like the change you've made. You must pay close attention, however, because you can only undo your very last command.

5. With the Category text box still selected, click the **Undo button** on the Report Design toolbar to remove the background color, click the **Line/Border Color list arrow** ·, then click the **blue box** (second row, third column from right)

6. Click the **Print Preview button** on the Report Design toolbar
   The screen should look like Figure D-15.

7. Click **File** on the menu bar, click **Print**, type **1** in the From text box, type **1** in the To text box, click **OK**, then click **Close** on the Print Preview toolbar
   The first page of the report is printed.

8. Click the **Save button**, then close the Quantities Report

FIGURE D-14: Working with color formats

Bold button

Fill/Back Color button

Font/Fore Color button

Category text box is selected

Line/Border Color button

Blue

Light gray

Red

FIGURE D-15: Formatted Quantities Report

Category text box has been formatted

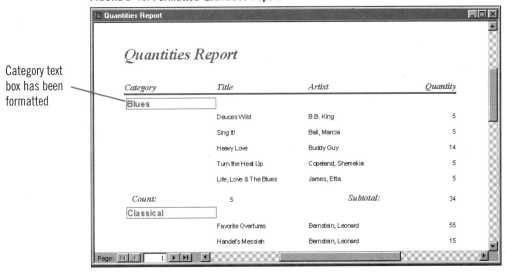

TABLE D-3: Popular formatting commands

button	button name	description
B	Bold	Toggles bold on or off for the selected control(s)
I	Italic	Toggles italics, on or off for the selected control(s)
U	Underline	Toggles underline on or off for the selected control(s)
≣	Align Left	Left-aligns the selected control(s) within its own border
≣	Center	Center-aligns the selected control(s) within its own border
≣	Align Right	Right-aligns the selected control(s) within its own border
◇ ▾	Fill/Back Color	Changes the background color of the selected control(s)
A ▾	Font/Fore Color	Changes the text color of the selected control(s)
✐ ▾	Line/Border Color	Changes the border color of the selected control(s)
▭ ▾	Line/Border Width	Changes the style of the border of the selected control(s)
▭ ▾	Special Effect	Changes the special visual effect of the selected control(s)

Creating Mailing Labels

Access 2000

Mailing Labels are used for many business purposes such as identifying paper folders and providing addresses for mass mailings. Once you enter raw data into your Access database, you can easily create mailing labels from this data using the **Label Wizard**. John has been asked to create labels for the display cases in the MediaLoft stores with the Artist and Title fields only. The labels are to be printed in alphabetical order by Artist and then by Title. John uses the Label Wizard to get started.

Steps

Trouble?

If you don't see Avery, click English units of measure, click the Filter by manufacturer list arrow, then click Avery.

1. Click **Reports** on the Objects bar in the MediaLoft-D Database window, click the **New button**, click **Label Wizard** in the New Report dialog box, click the **Choose the table or query where the object's data comes from list arrow**, click **Music Inventory**, then click **OK**

The Label Wizard dialog box opens requesting that you specify information about the characteristics of the label, as shown in Figure D-16. Avery 5160 labels are one of the most popular sizes. Avery 5160 label sheets have three columns and ten rows of labels for a total of 30 labels per page.

2. Click **5160**, then click **Next**

The next wizard dialog box allows you to change the font, font size, and other text attributes. Larger fonts will be easier to read and will fit on this label since there are only two fields of information.

Trouble?

If your system doesn't have the Comic Sans MS font, choose another font appropriate for music labels.

3. Click the **Font size list arrow**, click **11**, click the **Font name list arrow**, scroll and click **Comic Sans MS** (a sample appears in the Sample box), then click **Next**

The next wizard dialog box, which shows you the prototype label, allows you choose which fields you want to include in each label as well as their placement. Any spaces or punctuation that you want on the label must be entered from the keyboard. Also, if you want to put a field on a new line, you must press [Enter] to move to a new row of the prototype label.

QuickTip

You can double-click the field name in the Available Fields list to move it to the Prototype label list.

4. Click **Artist**, click the **Select Single Field button**, press **[Enter]**, click **Title**, then click

Your screen should look like Figure D-17.

5. Click **Next**

The next wizard dialog box asks about sorting.

6. Double-click **Artist** for your primary sort field, double-click **Title** for your secondary sort field, then click **Next**

You should give your labels a descriptive name.

7. Type **Artist-Title Labels** to name the report, click **Finish**, then click the **Zoom pointer** to see a full page of labels

The labels should look like Figure D-18.

8. Click **Close** on the Print Preview toolbar to see the Artist-Title Labels report in Design view, click the **Save button**, then click the **Print button**

9. Click **File** on the menu bar, then click **Exit** to exit Access

FIGURE D-16: Label Wizard

Avery 5160
label type

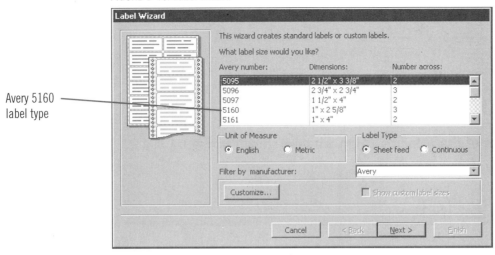

FIGURE D-17: The prototype label

Select Single Field
button

Artist field

Title field

FIGURE D-18: The Artist-Title Labels report

Labels are
3 columns by
10 rows on
each page

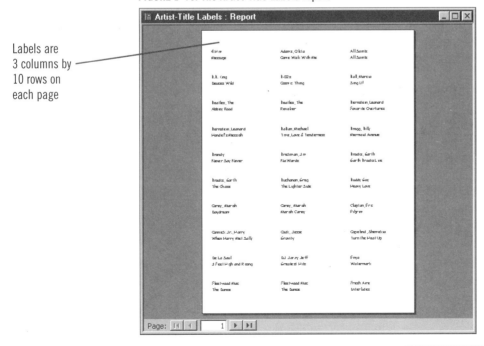

Practice

► Concepts Review

Label each element of the Report Design window shown in Figure D-19.

FIGURE D-19

Match each term with the statement that describes it.

8. **Function**	a. Part of the report that determines where a control will display on the report
9. **Section**	b. Sorting records *plus* providing a section before and after the group of records
10. **Detail section**	c. An Access object used to create paper printouts
11. **Report**	d. Enhancing the appearance of the information
12. **Formatting**	e. A built-in formula provided by Access that helps you quickly create a calculated expression
13. **Grouping**	f. Prints once for every record

Select the best answer from the list of choices.

14. **Press and hold which key to select more than one control in Report Design view?**
    a. [Ctrl]
    b. [Alt]
    c. [Shift]
    d. [Tab]

15. **Which type of control is most likely found in the Detail section?**
    a. Label
    b. Text box
    c. Combo box
    d. List box

16. **Which type of control is most likely found in the Page Header section?**
    a. Label
    b. Combo box
    c. Command button
    d. Bound image

17. **A calculated expression is most often found in which report section?**
    a. Report Header
    b. Detail
    c. Formulas
    d. Group Footer

18. **Which of the following would be the appropriate expression to count the number of records using the FirstName field?**
    a. =Count(FirstName)
    b. =Count[FirstName)
    c. =Count{FirstName}
    d. =Count([FirstName])

19. **To align the edges of several controls with respect to one another, you use the alignment commands on the**
    a. Formatting toolbar.
    b. Standard toolbar.
    c. Print Preview toolbar.
    d. Format menu.

► Skills Review

1. Plan a report.

a. Pretend that you are looking for a job. Plan a report to use for tracking job opportunities. To gather the raw data for your report, find a newspaper with job listings in your area of interest.

b. Identify the Report Header, Group Header, and Detail sections of the report by using sample data based on the following information:

- The title of the report should be "Job Opportunity Report."
- The records should be grouped by job title. For example, if you are interested in working with computers, job titles might be "Computer Operator" or "Computer Analyst." Include at least two job title groupings in your sample report.
- The Detail section should include information on the company, contact, and telephone number for each job opportunity.

2. Create a report.

a. Start Access and open the Club-D database on your Project Disk.

b. Use the Report Wizard to create a report based on the Contacts table.

c. Include the following fields for the report:
STATUS, FNAME, LNAME, DUESOWED, DUESPAID

d. Do not add any grouping or sorting fields.

e. Use the Tabular layout and Portrait orientation.

f. Use a bold style and title the report "Contact Status Report."

g. Preview the first page of the new report.

3. Group records.

a. In Report Design view, open the Sorting and Grouping dialog box, and group the report by the STATUS field in ascending order. Open both the Group Header and Group Footer sections, then close the dialog box.

b. Move the STATUS text box in the Detail section up to the left edge of the STATUS Header section.

c. Preview the first page of the new report.

4. Change the sort order.

a. In Report Design view, open the Sorting and Grouping dialog box, then add LNAME as a sort field in ascending order immediately below the STATUS field.

b. Preview the first page of the new report.

5. Modify an expression.

a. In Report Design view, add a text box control in the STATUS Footer section directly below the DUESOWED text box in the Detail section.

b. Delete the accompanying label to the left of the unbound text box.

c. Add a text box control in the STATUS Footer section directly below the DUESPAID text box in the Detail section.

d. Delete the accompanying label to the left of the unbound text box by clicking the label, then pressing [Delete].

e. Add an unbound label to the report header, and type your name as the label.

f. Modify the text boxes so that they subtotal the DUESOWED and DUESPAID fields respectively. The calculated expressions will be =Sum([DUESOWED]) and =Sum([DUESPAID]).

g. Preview both pages of the report, then print both pages of the report.

6. **Align controls.**
   a. In Report Design view, right-align the new calculated controls in the STATUS Footer section.
   b. Select the DUESOWED text box in the Detail section, and the =Sum([DUESOWED]) calculated expression in the STATUS Footer, then right-align the controls with respect to one another.
   c. Select the DUESPAID text box in the Detail section, and the =Sum([DUESPAID]) calculated expression in the STATUS Footer, then right-align the controls with respect to one another.

7. **Format controls.**
   a. Select the two calculated controls in the STATUS Footer, click the Properties button, then change the Format property on the Format tab to Currency. Close the property sheet.
   b. Select the STATUS text box in the STATUS Header section, change the font size to 12 points, bold and italicize the control, then change the background color to bright yellow.
   c. Preview the report, check the new totals, save the report, print it, then close the report.

8. **Create mailing labels.**
   a. Use the Label Wizard and the Contacts table to create mailing labels using Avery 5160 labels.
   b. The text should be formatted as Arial, 10 points, Light font weight, black, with no italic or underline attributes.
   c. The prototype label should be organized as follows:
      FNAME LNAME
      COMPANY
      STREET
      CITY, STATE ZIP
   d. Sort the labels by the ZIP field.
   e. Name the report "Mailing Labels."
   f. Print the first page of the labels, save the report, then close it.
   g. Exit Access.

▶ Independent Challenges

1. You have been hired to create several reports for a physical therapy clinic.
To complete this independent challenge:

a. Start Access and open the Therapy-D database from your Project Disk.

b. Using the Report Wizard, create a report using all of the fields from the Location Financial Query.

c. View your data by Survey, group by Street, sort in ascending order by PatientLast, and sum both the AmountSent and AmountRecorded fields.

d. Use the Stepped layout, Portrait orientation, and Soft Gray style.

e. Name the report "Location Financial Report."

f. Modify the AmountSent and AmountRecorded labels in the Page Header section to "Sent" and "Recorded" respectively.

g. Change the font/fore color of the labels in the Page Header section to bright blue.

h. Widen the Street text box label in the Street Header section to twice its current size, and change the border color to bright blue.

i. Save and print the report.

j. Exit Access.

2. You have been hired to create several reports for a physical therapy clinic.
To complete this independent challenge:

a. Start Access and open the Therapy-D database from your Project Disk.

b. Using the Report Wizard, create a report using all of the fields from the Therapist Satisfaction Query except for the Initials and First fields.

c. View the data by Survey. Do not add any grouping levels and do not add any sorting levels.

d. Use the Tabular layout, Portrait orientation, and Casual style.

e. Title the report "Therapist Satisfaction Report," then print the report.

f. In Report Design view, group the report by Last, and open both the Group Header and Group Footer sections.

g. Further sort the records by PatientLast.

h. Move the Last text box from the Detail section up into the Last Header section.

i. Remove bold from all of the labels in the Page Header section.

j. Add text boxes in the Last Footer section directly below the Courtesy and Knowledge text boxes in the Detail section. Enter the calculated controls =Avg([Courtesy]) and =Avg([Knowledge]) respectively. Delete their accompanying labels, and resize the new calculated controls so that they are a little narrower than the Courtesy and Knowledge text boxes in the Detail section.

k. Open the property sheet for the two new calculated controls, and change the Format property on the Format tab to "Fixed."

l. Right-align the two new calculated controls within their own borders. Also, align the right edge of the =Avg([Courtesy]) control with respect to the Courtesy text box in the Detail section. Right-align the edges of the =Avg([Knowledge]) and Knowledge text boxes with respect to each other.

m. Align the top edges of the new calculated controls.

n. Drag the right edge of the report to the left so the report is 6½" wide (if necessary).

o. Save, preview, and print the report.

p. Exit Access.

3. Use the knowledge and skills that you have acquired about Access to create an attractive report that includes information about colleges and universities that offer programs in computer science. Create a database containing this information, and then design a report that displays the data. Gather information from libraries, friends, and the Web to enter into the database.

To complete this independent challenge:

a. Start Access and create a new database called "Colleges" on your Project Disk. Include any fields you feel are important, but make sure you include the institution's name, state, and whether it is a 4- or 2-year school.

b. Find information on schools that offer programs in computer science. If you are using the Web, use any available search engines.

c. Compile a list of at least 15 institutions, and enter the 15 records into a table named "Computer Science Schools."

d. Create a report that includes all the fields in the table Computer Science Schools, and group by the field that contains the information on whether it is a 4- or 2-year school.

e. Sort the records in ascending order by the state, then by the institution's name.

f. Use an appropriate style and title for your report. Insert your initials at the end of the report title so you can identify it.

g. Save, preview, and print the report.

h. Exit Access.

4. As an assistant in the marketing department at MediaLoft, you are often asked to create mailing labels for the MediaLoft store locations. You have decided to create a small database that stores information about the stores so that you can quickly create the labels using the Label Wizard.

To complete this independent challenge:

a. Start Access and create a new database on your Project Disk called "MediaLoft Locations."

b. Connect to the Internet, use your browser to go to the MediaLoft intranet site at http://www.course.com/illustrated/MediaLoft, then click the About link for the page with the MediaLoft store locations.

c. Print the Web page that displays the store locations.

d. Disconnect from the Internet, and switch to the Access window.

e. Create a table called "Stores" with the following fields (each field's data type should be Text):
StoreName, Street, City, State, Zip, Phone

f. Using the Stores datasheet, type each store location into the database. Pay close attention to capitalization and spelling.

g. Using the Label Wizard, create mailing labels with the store address information on Avery 5160 labels.

h. Format the label with any decorative font, a 12-point font size, and bright red text.

i. Use the following label prototype:
StoreName
Street
City, State Zip

j. Name the label report "Store Address Labels," and print the report.

k. Save and close the report, then exit Access.

▶ Visual Workshop

Use the Club-D database on your Project Disk to create the report based on the CONTACTS table shown in Figure D-20. The Report Wizard and the Corporate style were used to create this report. Note that the records are grouped by the CITY field and sorted within each group by the LNAME field. A calculated control that counts the number of records is displayed in the Group Footer.

FIGURE D-20

Membership by City

CITY	LNAME	FNAME	PHONE
Bridgewater			
	Daniels	Mark	555-2277
Count: 1			
Fontanelle			
	Eagan	Jane	555-1166
Count: 1			
Industrial Airport			
	Braven	Mary	555-7002
Count: 1			
Kansas City			
	Alman	Jill	555-6931
	Bouchart	Bob	555-3081
	Collins	Christine	555-3602
	Diverman	Barbara	555-0401
	Duman	Mary Jane	555-8844
	Eahle	Andrea	555-0401
	Eckert	Jay	555-7414
	Hammer	Mike	555-0365
	Hubert	Holly	555-6004
	Mackintosh	Helen	555-9414
	Mayberry	Mitch	555-0401
	Olson	Marcie	555-1388
	Parton	Jeanette	555-8773
	Walker	Shirley	555-0403
Count: 14			

Access 2000 MOUS Certification Objectives

Below is a list of the Microsoft™ Office User Specialist program objectives for Core Access 2000 skills showing where each MOUS objective is covered in the Lessons and Practice. This table lists the Core MOUS certification skills covered in the units in this book (Units A-D). The remaining core skills are covered in *Microsoft Office 2000—Illustrated Second Course* (Units E-H). For more information on which Illustrated titles meet MOUS certification, please see the inside cover of this book.

MOUS standardized coding number	Activity	Lesson page where skill is covered	Location in lesson where skill is covered	Practice
AC2000.1	**Planning and designing databases**			
AC2000.1.1	Determine appropriate data inputs for your database	Access A-3 Access B-2	Figure A-1, A-2 Details Table B-1	Skills Review, Independent Challenges 1-4, Visual Workshop
AC2000.1.2	Determine appropriate data outputs for your database	Access A-4	Table A-2	Skills Review, Independent Challenges 1-4
AC2000.1.3	Create table structure	Access B-4	Steps 2-7	Skills Review, Independent Challenges 1-4
AC2000.1.4	Establish table relationships			
AC2000.2	**Working with Access**			
AC2000.2.1	Use the Office Assistant	Access A-18	Steps 3-6	Skills review
AC2000.2.2	Select an object using the Objects Bar	Access A-8 Access B-8 Access C-6 Access D-8	Steps 5-6 Steps 1-2 Step 1 Step 1	Skills Review, Independent Challenges 1-4
AC2000.2.3	Print database objects (tables, forms, reports, queries)	Access A-16 Access C-14 Access C-16	Steps 1-7 Step 7 Step 8	Skills Review, Independent Challenges 1-4
AC2000.2.4	Navigate through records in a table, query, or form	Access A-10 Access C-14	Steps 2-6 Steps 3-5	Skills Review, Independent Challenges 1-4
AC2000.2.5	Create a database (using a Wizard or in Design View)			
AC2000.3	**Building and modifying tables**			
AC2000.3.1	Create tables by using the Table Wizard	Access B-4	Step 1	Skills Review, Independent Challenges 1-2
AC2000.3.2	Set primary keys	Access B-4	Steps 6-7	Skills Review, Independent Challenges 1-4
AC2000.3.3	Modify field properties	Access B-6	Steps 5-6	Skills Review, Independent Challenges 1-4
AC2000.3.4	Use multiple data types	Access B-6	Step 2	Skills Review, Independent Challenges 1-4
AC2000.3.5	Modify tables using Design View	Access B-6	Steps 1-8	Skills Review, Independent Challenges 1-4
AC2000.3.6	Use the Lookup Wizard			
AC2000.3.7	Use the input mask wizard			
AC2000.4	**Building and modifying forms**			
AC2000.4.1	Create a form with the Form Wizard	Access C-4	Steps 1-3	Skills Review, Independent Challenges 1-3

MOUS standardized coding number	Activity	Lesson page where skill is covered	Location in lesson where skill is covered	Practice
AC2000.4.2	Use the Control Toolbox to add controls	Access C-10 Access C-16	Steps 1-7 Steps 2-5	Skills Review, Independent Challenges 2-3
AC2000.4.3	Modify Format Properties (font, style, font size, color, caption, etc.) of controls	Access C-8 Access C-10	Steps 2-5 Steps 5-6	Skills Review, Independent Challenges 2-3
AC2000.4.4	Use form sections (headers, footers, detail)	Access C-6 Access C-12 Access C-16	Steps 1-6 Steps 2-5 Steps 2-5	Skills Review, Independent Challenges 2-3
AC2000.4.5	Use a Calculated Control on a form	Access C-10	Steps 2-7	Skills Review, Independent Challenges 2
AC2000.5	**Viewing and organizing information**			
AC2000.5.1	Use the Office Clipboard	Access D-10	Clues to Use	Skills Review, Independent Challenges 2-3
AC2000.5.2	Switch between object Views	Access B-6 Access B-18 Access C-10 Access D-8	Step 7 Step 6 Step 8	Skills Review, Independent Challenges 1-4, Visual Workshop
AC2000.5.3	Enter records using a datasheet	Access A-12	Steps 2-4	Skills Review, Independent Challenges 3-4, Visual Workshop
AC2000.5.4	Enter records using a form	Access C-14	Step 2	Skills Review, Independent Challenge 1, Visual Workshop
AC2000.5.5	Delete records from a table	Access A-14	Step 9	Skills Review
AC2000.5.6	Find a record	Access B-10 Access B-14 Access C-14	Details Steps 4-8 Steps 4-6	Skills Review, Independent Challenge 1, Visual Workshop
AC2000.5.7	Sort records	Access B-10 Access B-12 Access C-6 Access D-8	Steps 1-3 Details Step 7 Steps 1-5	Skills Review, Independent Challenges 1-4
AC2000.5.8	Apply and remove filters (filter by form and filter by selection)	Access B-10 Access B-14	Details Steps 1-6	Skills Review
AC2000.5.9	Specify criteria in a query	Access B-16 Access B-18	Step 6 Step 4	Skills Review, Independent Challenges 1-4, Visual Workshop
AC2000.5.10	Display related records in a subdatasheet			
AC2000.5.11	Create a calculated field	Access C-10	Steps 1-6	Skills Review, Independent Challenge 3
AC2000.5.12	Create and modify a multi-table select query			
AC2000.6	**Defining relationships**			
AC2000.6.1	Establish relationships			
AC2000.6.2	Enforce referential integrity			
AC2000.7	**Producing reports**			
AC2000.7.1	Create a report with the Report Wizard	Access D-4	Steps 2-5	Skills Review, Independent Challenges 1-4, Visual Workshop

MOUS standardized coding number	Activity	Lesson page where skill is covered	Location in lesson where skill is covered	Practice
AC2000.7.2	Preview and print a report	Access D-6	Step 7	Skills Review, Independent Challenges 1-4, Visual Workshop
AC2000.7.3	Move and resize a control	Access D-12	Steps 2-5	Skills Review, Independent Challenges 1-4, Visual Workshop
AC2000.7.4	Modify format properties (font, style, font size, color, caption, etc.)	Access D-14	Steps 2-7	Skills Review, Independent Challenges 1-4, Visual Workshop
AC2000.7.5	Use the Control Toolbox to add controls	Access D-6	Steps 3-6	Skills Review, Independent Challenges 1-4, Visual Workshop
AC2000.7.6	Use report sections (headers, footers, detail)	Access D-3 Access D-6	Table D-1, Figure D-5 Steps 1-7	Skills Review, Independent Challenges 1-4, Visual Workshop
AC2000.7.7	Use a Calculated Control in a report	Access D-12	Step 4	Skills Review, Independent Challenge 1
AC2000.8	**Integrating with other applications**			
AC2000.8.1	Import data to a new table			
AC2000.8.2	Save a table, query, form as a Web page			
AC2000.8.3	Add Hyperlinks			
AC2000.9	**Using Access Tools**			
AC2000.9.1	Print Database Relationships			
AC2000.9.2	Backup and Restore a database			
AC2000.9.3	Compact and Repair a database			

Glossary

And criteria Criteria placed in the same row of the query design grid. All criteria on the same row must be true in order for a record to appear on the resulting datasheet.

Arguments The pieces of information a function needs to create the final answer. In an expression, multiple arguments are separated by commas. All of the arguments are surrounded by a single set of parentheses.

Ascending order A sequence in which information is placed in alphabetical order or from smallest to largest. For a text field, numbers sort first, then letters.
Text ascending order: 123, 3H, 455, 98, 98B, animal, Iowa, New Jersey
Date ascending order: 1/1/57, 1/1/61, 12/25/61, 5/5/98, 8/20/98, 8/20/99
Number ascending order: 1, 10, 15, 120, 140, 500, 1200, 1500

AutoNumber A data type in which Access enters a sequential integer for each record added into the datasheet. Numbers cannot be reused even if the record is deleted.

Bound control A control used in either a form or report to display data from the underlying record source; also used to edit and enter new data in a form.

Bound image control A bound control used to show OLE data such as a picture on a form or report.

Calculated control A control that uses information from existing controls to calculate new data such as subtotals, dates, or page numbers; used in either a form or report.

Caption property A field property used to override the technical field name with an easy-to-read caption entry when the field name appears* on datasheets, forms, and reports.

Check box Bound control used to display "yes" or "no" answers for a field. If the box is "checked" it indicates "yes" information in a form or report.

Clipboard toolbar A toolbar that shows the contents of the Office Clipboard; contains buttons for copying and pasting items to and from the Office Clipboard.

Combo box A bound control used to display a list of possible entries for a field in which you can also type an entry from the keyboard. It is a "combination" of the list box and text box controls.

Command button An unbound control used to provide an easy way to initiate an action or run a macro.

Control Any element on a form or report such as a label, text box, line, or combo box. Controls can be bound, unbound, or calculated.

Criteria The entry that determines which records are displayed when finding or filtering records in a datasheet or form, or when building a query.

Currency A data type used for monetary values.

Current record symbol A black triangle symbol that appears in the record select box to the left of the record that has the focus in either a datasheet or a form.

Data The unique entries of information that you enter into the fields of the records.

Data Access Page See "Page".

Database A collection of data associated with a topic (for example, sales of products to customers).

Database software Software used to manage data that can be organized into lists of things such as customers, products, vendors, employees, projects, or sales.

Database window The window that includes common elements such as the Access title bar, menu bar, and toolbar. It also contains an Objects bar to quickly work with the seven different types of objects within the database by clicking the appropriate object button.

Datasheet A spreadsheet-like grid that shows fields as columns and records as rows.

Datasheet view A view that lists the records of the object in a datasheet. Table, query, and most form objects have a Datasheet view.

Data type A required property for each field that defines the type of data that can be entered in each field. Valid data types include AutoNumber, Text, Number, Currency, Date/Time, OLE Object, Memo, Yes/No, and Hyperlink.

Date/Time A data type used for date and time fields.

Descending order A sequence in which information is placed in reverse alphabetical order or from largest to smallest. For a text field, letters sort first, then numbers.
Text descending order: Zebra, Victory, Langguth, Bunin, 99A, 9854, 77, 740, 29, 270, 23500, 1
Date descending order: 1/1/99, 1/1/98, 12/25/97, 5/5/97, 8/20/61, 8/20/57
Number descending order: 1500, 1400, 1200, 140, 120, 15, 10, 1

Design view A view in which the structure of the object can be manipulated. Every Access object has a Design view.

Detail section The section of the form or report that contains the controls that are printed for each record in the underlying query or table.

Edit mode The mode in which Access assumes you are trying to edit that particular field, so keystrokes such as [Ctrl][End], [Ctrl][Home], [¨], and [Æ] move the insertion point within the field.

Edit record symbol A pencil-like symbol that appears in the record selector box to the left of the record that is currently being edited in either a datasheet or a form.

Expression A combination of values, functions, and operators that calculates to a single value. Access expressions start with an equal sign and are placed in a text box in either Form or Report Design view.

Field The smallest piece or category of information in a database such as the customer's name, city, state, or phone number.

Field list A list of the available fields in the table or query that it represents.

Field names The names given each field in Table Design or Table Datasheet view. Field names can be up to 64 characters long.

Field Property See *Properties*.

Filter A temporary view of a subset of records. A filter can be saved as a query object if you wish to apply the same filter later without recreating it.

Filter window A window that appears when you click the Filter by Form button when viewing data in a datasheet or in a form window. The Filter window allows you to define the filter criteria.

Focus The property that refers to which field would be edited if you started typing.

Footer Information that prints at the bottom of every printed page (or section when using forms and reports).

Form An Access object that provides an easy-to-use data entry screen that generally shows only one record at a time.

Formatting Enhancing the appearance of the information in a form, report or datasheet.

Form Design toolbar The toolbar that appears when working in Form Design View with buttons that help you modify a form's controls.

Form View toolbar The toolbar that appears when working in Form View with buttons that help you print, edit, find, filter, and edit records.

Function A special, predefined formula that provides a shortcut for a commonly used calculation, for example, AVERAGE.

Graphic See *Image*.

Group Footer section The section of the report that contains controls that print once at the end of each group of records.

Group Header section The section of the report that contains controls that print once at the beginning of each group of records.

Handles See *Sizing handles*.

Header Information that prints at the top of every printed page (or section when using forms and reports).

Help system Pages of documentation and examples that are available through the Help menu option, the Microsoft Access Help button on the Database toolbar, or the Office Assistant.

Hyperlink A data type that stores World Wide Web addresses.

Image A nontextual piece of information such as a picture, piece of clip art, drawn object, or graph. Because images are graphical (not numbers or letters), they are sometimes referred to as *graphical images*.

Key field A field that contains unique information for each record. Also known as *Primary key field*. A key field cannot contain a null entry.

Key field symbol In a table's Design view, the symbol that appears as a miniature key in the field indicator box to the left of the field name. It identifies the field that contains unique information for each record.

Label An unbound control that displays static text on forms and reports.

Line control An unbound control used to draw lines on a form or report that divide it into logical groupings.

List box A bound control that displays a list of possible choices from which the user can choose. Used mainly on forms.

Lookup wizard Specifying a lookup data type for a field invokes a wizard that helps link the current table to another table. The final data type of the field is determined by choices made in the wizard. A field created with the lookup data type will consist of data from another table or list.

Macro An Access object that stores a collection of keystrokes or commands such as printing several reports in a row or providing a toolbar when a form opens.

Memo A data type used for lengthy text such as comments or notes. It can hold up to 64,000 characters of information.

Module An Access object that stores Visual Basic programming code that extends the functions and automated processes of Access.

Navigation buttons Buttons in the lower-left corner of a datasheet or form that allow you to quickly navigate between the records in the underlying object as well as add a new record.

Navigation mode A mode in which Access assumes that you are trying to move between the fields and records of the datasheet (rather than edit a specific field's contents), so keystrokes such as [Ctrl][Home] and [Ctrl][End] move you to the first and last field of the datasheet, respectively.

New Record button A button that, when clicked, presents a new record for data entry. It is found on both the Form View and Datasheet toolbars as well as part of the Navigation buttons.

Null The term that refers to a state of "nothingness" in a field. Any entry such as 0 in a numeric field or an invisible space in a text field is *not* null. It is common to search for empty fields by using the criteria "Is Null" in a filter or query. "Is Not Null" criteria finds all records where there is an entry of any kind.

Number A data type used for numeric information used in calculations, such as quantities.

Object A table, query, form, report, page, macro, or module.

Objects bar In the opening database window, the toolbar that presents the seven Access objects. When you click an object button on the Objects bar, options and wizards to create an object of that type as well as existing objects of that type appear in the main portion of the database window.

Office Assistant An animated character that appears to offer tips, answer questions, and provide access to the program's Help system.

Office Clipboard A temporary storage area shared by all Office programs that can be used to cut, copy and paste multiple items within and between Office programs. The Office Clipboard can hold up to 12 items collected from any Office program. See also *Clipboard toolbar*.

OLE Object A data type that stores pointers that tie files created in other programs to a record such as pictures, sound clips, word-processing documents, or spreadsheets.

Option button A bound control used to display a limited list of possible choices for field such as "female" or "male" for a gender field in a form or report.

Or criteria Criteria placed on different rows of the query design grid. A record will appear in the resulting datasheet if it is true for any single row.

Page An Access object that creates Web pages from Access objects as well as provides Web page connectivity features to an Access database. Also called Data Access Page.

Page Footer section The section of the form or report that contains controls that print once at the bottom of each page.

Page Header section The section of the form or report that contains controls that print once at the top of each page. On the first page of the report, the Page Header section prints below the Report Header section.

Primary key field See *Key field*.

Primary sort field In a query grid, the left-most field that includes sort criteria. It determines the order in which the records will appear and can be specified "ascending" or "descending."

Print Preview A window that displays how the physical printout will appear if the current object is printed.

Properties Characteristics that further define the field (if field properties), control (if control properties), section (if section properties), or object (if object properties).

Property sheet A window that displays an exhaustive list of properties for the chosen control, section, or object within the form or report Design view.

Query An Access object which provides a spreadsheet-like view of the data similar to tables. It may provide the user with a subset of fields and/or records from one or more tables. Queries are created when a user has a "question" about the data in the database.

Raw data The individual pieces of information stored in the database in individual fields.

Record A group of related fields, such as all demographic information for one customer.

Record selector box The small square to left of a record in a datasheet that marks the current record or edit record symbol when the record has focus or is being edited. Clicking the record selector box selects the entire record. In Form view, the record selector box expands to the entire height of the form because only one record is viewed at a time.

Record source In a form or report, either a table or query object that contains the fields and records that the form will display. It is the most important property of the form or report object. A bound control on a form or report also has a record source property. In this case, the record source property identifies the field to which the control is bound.

Rectangle control An unbound control used to draw rectangles on the form that divide the other form controls into logical groupings.

Relational database A database in which more than one table, such as the customer, sales, and inventory tables, can share information. The term "relational database" comes from the fact that the tables are linked or "related" with a common field of information. An Access database is relational.

Report An Access object which creates a professional printout of data that may contain such enhancements as headers, footers, and calculations on groups of records.

Report Footer section On a report, a section that contains controls that print once at the end of the last page of the report.

Report Header section On a report, a section that contains controls that print once at the top of the first page of the report.

Row selector The small square to the left of a field in Table Design view.

ScreenTip A pop-up label that appears when you point to a button. It provides descriptive information about the button.

Secondary sort field In a query grid, the second field from the left that includes sort criteria. It determines the order in which the records will appear if there is a "tie" on the primary sort field. (For example, the primary sort field might be the State field. If two records both contained the data "IA" in that field, the secondary sort field, which might be the City field, would determine the order of the IA records in the resulting datasheet.)

Section A location of a form or report that contains controls. The section in which a control is placed determines where and how often the control prints.

Sizing handles Small squares at each corner of a selected control. Dragging a handle resizes the control. Also known as *handles*.

Sort To place records in an order (ascending or descending) based on the values of a particular field.

Source document The original paper document that records raw data such as an employment application. In some databases, there is no source document because raw data is entered directly into the computer.

Specific record box Part of the Navigation buttons that indicates the current record number. You can also click in the specific record box and type a record number to quickly move to that record.

Status bar The bar at the bottom of the Access window that provides informational messages and other status information (such as whether the Num Lock is active or not).

Tab control An unbound control used to create a three-dimensional aspect to a form so that other controls can be organized and shown in Form view by clicking the "tabs."

Tab order The sequence in which the controls on the form receive the focus when pressing [Tab] or [Enter] in Form view.

Table An Access object which is a collection of records for a single subject, such as all of the customer records. Tables can be linked with a common field to share information and therefore minimize data redundancy.

Table Datasheet toolbar The toolbar that appears when you are viewing a table's datasheet.

Text A data type that allows text information or combinations of text and numbers such as a street address. By default, it is 50 characters but can be changed to 50 characters. The maximum length of a text field is 255 characters.

Text box A common control used on forms and reports to display data bound to an underlying field. A text box can also show calculated controls such as subtotals and dates.

Toggle button A bound control used to indicate "yes" or "no" answers for a field. If the button is "pressed" it displays "yes" information.

Toolbox toolbar The toolbar that has common controls that you can add to a report or form when working in the report or form's Design view.

Unbound controls Controls that do not change from record to record and exist only to clarify or enhance the appearance of the form, such as labels, lines, and clip art.

Unbound image control An unbound control used to display clip art that doesn't change as you navigate from record to record on a form or report.

Wildcard characters Special characters used in criteria to find, filter, and query data. The asterisk (*) stands for any group of characters. For example, the criteria I* in a State field criteria cell would find all records where the state entry was IA, ID, IL, IN, or Iowa. The question mark (?) wildcard stands for only one character. The pound sign (#) can only be used as a wildcard in a numeric field and stands for a single number.

Wizard An interactive set of dialog boxes that guides you through an Access process such as creating a query, form, or report.

Yes/No A data type that stores only one of two values (Yes/No, On/Off, True/False).

Index

Index